W9-BUL-815

CHARLES HARTSHORNE

Makers of the Modern Theological Mind

Bob E. Patterson, Editor

KARL BARTH by *David L. Mueller*
DIETRICH BONHOEFFER by *Dallas M. Roark*
RUDOLF BULTMANN by *Morris Ashcraft*
CHARLES HARTSHORNE by *Alan Gragg*
WOLFHART PANNENBERG by *Don Olive*
TEILHARD DE CHARDIN by *Doran McCarty*
EMIL BRUNNER by *J. Edward Humphrey*
MARTIN BUBER by *Stephen M. Panko*
SÖREN KIERKEGAARD by *Elmer H. Duncan*
REINHOLD NIEBUHR by *Bob E. Patterson*
H. RICHARD NIEBUHR by *Lonnie D. Kliever*
GERHARD VON RAD by *James L. Crenshaw*
ANDERS NYGREN by *Thor Hall*
FRIEDRICH SCHLEIERMACHER by *C. W. Christian*
HANS KÜNG by *John Kiwiet*
IAN T. RAMSEY by *William Williamson*
CARL F. H. HENRY by *Bob E. Patterson*
PAUL TILLICH by *John Newport*

Makers of the Modern Theological Mind

Bob E. Patterson, Editor

CHARLES HARTSHORNE

Alan Gragg

PEABODY, MASSACHUSETTS 01961-3473

CHARLES HARTSHORNE

Copyright © 1973
Hendrickson Publishers, Inc.
P.O. Box 3473
Peabody, Massachusetts 01961-3473
Printed in the United States of America

ISBN 0-943575-62-1

Grateful acknowledgment is made to the following publishers for permission to quote from copyrighted material:

Open Court Publishing Company, LaSalle, Ill., for quotations from Charles Hartshorne, *The Logic of Perfection and Other Essays in Neo-classical Metaphysics* (1962), and *A Natural Theology for Our Time* (1967).

University of Chicago Press, Chicago, Ill., for quotations from Charles Hartshorne, *The Philosophy and Psychology of Sensation*, copyright 1934 The University of Chicago Press.

University of Nebraska Press, Lincoln, Neb., for quotations from Charles Hartshorne, *Beyond Humanism: Essays in the Philosophy of Nature* (1968).

Yale University Press, New Haven, Conn., for quotations from Charles Hartshorne, *The Divine Relativity: A Social Conception of God* (1948).

Library of Congress Cataloging-in-Publication Data

Gragg, Alan.
    Charles Hartshorne / by Alan Gragg.
      p. cm.
    Reprint. Originally published: Waco, Tex.: Word Books, c1973. (Makers of the modern theological mind).
    Includes bibliographical references.
    ISBN 0-943575-62-1
    1. Hartshorne, Charles, 1897- .   I. Title. II. Series: Makers of the modern theological mind.
    [B945.H354G72 1991]
    210'.92-dc20   90-29860
                                           CIP

Dedicated to
ROBERT E. CUSHMAN
my mentor in
philosophical theology

Contents

Editor's Preface

Who are the thinkers that have shaped Christian theology in our time? This series tries to answer that question by providing a reliable guide to the ideas of the men who have significantly charted the theological seas of our century. In the current revival of theology, these books will give a new generation the opportunity to be exposed to significant minds. They are not meant, however, to be a substitute for a careful study of the original works of these makers of the modern theological mind.

This series is not for the lazy. Each major theologian is examined carefully and critically—his life, his theological method, his most germinal ideas, his weaknesses as a thinker, his place in the theological spectrum, and his chief contribution to the climate of theology today. The books are written with the assumption that laymen will read them and enter into the theological dialogue that is so necessary to the church as a whole. At the same time they are carefully enough designed to give assurance to a Ph.D. student in theology preparing for his preliminary exams.

Each author in the series is a professional scholar and theologian in his own right. All are specialists on, and in some cases have studied with, the theologians about whom they write. Welcome to the series.

Bob E. Patterson, Editor
Baylor University

I. The Career of
Charles Hartshorne

"My position is that the non-theist lacks thoroughness and clarity in the intellectual framework of his position."
—"Is God's Existence a State of Affairs?"

Charles Hartshorne (pronounced "harts-horn") is a distinguished professor of philosophy in The University of Texas at Austin. One of the most eminent of living American philosophers, Hartshorne has had a career that may be easily sketched. He was born in Kittanning, Pennsylvania, in 1897, the son of a clergyman, the Reverend F. C. Hartshorne. Charles remembers his father along with Professor Rufus M. Jones and an unnamed science teacher as the pivotal influences of his childhood and youth, who instilled in him a religious reverence for intellectual integrity.[1]

Hartshorne attended Haverford College for two years (1915–17), but his college education was interrupted by two years of service in the United States Army (1917–19) in the role of a hospital orderly. Resuming his academic training at Harvard University, he earned the A.B. degree in 1921, the A.M. degree in 1922, and the Ph.D. degree in 1923. After winning his doctorate with a dissertation on "The Unity of Being," he spent two years (1923–25) in Europe, primarily at the Universities of Freiburg and Mar-

burg, where he studied with the famous phenomenologist
Edmund Husserl and the great existentialist Martin Heidegger.[2] During the years 1925–28, Hartshorne was back
at Harvard as a research fellow, serving for one semester
as assistant to the renowned British-American philosopher
Alfred North Whitehead.

Hartshorne's professorial odyssey has taken him as professor of philosophy mainly to three American universities:
The University of Chicago, 1928–55, including the Fed-
erated Theological Faculty from 1943 to 1955; Emory
University, 1955–62; and The University of Texas, from
1962 until the present. Moreover, he has held visiting pro-
fessorships or special lectureships at Stanford University,
New School for Social Research; the University of Wash-
ington; Yale University; Frankfurt, Germany; Melbourne,
Australia; and Kyoto, Japan.

Although he is comparatively small in physical stature,
Hartshorne is one of the giant intellects in contemporary
philosophy. He gladly acknowledges his intellectual indebtedness and kinship to other philosophical minds of
past and present, but he is no merely eclectic thinker. His
rational powers display remarkable penetration, steady intensity, and some notable originality and independence. In
general philosophical terms, Hartshorne may properly be
called an untamed rationalist. His serene confidence in the
powers of philosophical rationality, when disciplined by
logical rigor, to discover and describe the major facets of
ultimate reality radiates from his speeches and writings.
He reports that, after reading Emerson's *Essays* at about
the age of seventeen, he resolved "to trust reason to the
end"; and, therefore, he has sought to make his "thinking
about metaphysical and religious questions good thinking,

good by the proper criteria of thinking, rather than of per-
suading, edifying, or expressing emotion." [3] Hartshorne's
readers soon discover that the effort to comprehend his
thought is not only an exciting intellectual adventure but
also an arduous mental task.

Regarding his intellectual affinities, Hartshorne feels
himself to be "closest" to Charles Sanders Peirce, Henri
Bergson, and A. N. Whitehead.[4] He expresses gratitude to
his Harvard professors C. I. Lewis and H. M. Sheffer for
introducing him to "logical exactitude," and especially to
Professor William Ernest Hocking, his first teacher in philosophical theology, for fresh insights into a philosophically
trustworthy vision of God.[5] Furthermore, he acknowledges
some indebtedness to Josiah Royce, William James, and
Ralph Barton Perry, as well as a close kinship to the Rus-
sian existentialist Nicolai Berdyaev.[6] Nevertheless, Hartshorne's philosophy is strikingly similar and most profoundly indebted to that of A. N. Whitehead. Though
Hartshorne developed some of his Whiteheadian notions
before he encountered Whitehead, his mature philosophy
may not improperly be described as an original adaptation
of Whitehead's philosophical cosmology and theology.
Hartshorne does not hesitate to modify (often for the better) and even reject some of Whitehead's views, but the
influence of Whitehead's metaphysics upon Hartshorne's
metaphysics is unmistakably all-pervasive. Indeed, it is
well-nigh impossible to imagine Hartshorne apart from
Whitehead. Therefore, one may much more easily comprehend the intricacies of Hartshorne's philosophy if he already commands a general understanding of Whitehead.

What is the place of Charles Hartshorne in twentieth-
century American theology and philosophy? Any compre-

hensive assessment of the depth and scope of his influence
at this time would be decidedly premature. In some intellectual quarters, he is just beginning to receive the attention
his meticulous thought deserves; and it is hoped that this
brief study will help enlarge still further the ever-widening
range of his impact. Moreover, it is even now possible to
say that Hartshorne's strenuous mental labors have not
been in vain, for he has already made a decisive mark upon
contemporary American philosophy and theology.

Though Hartshorne considers himself primarily a philosophical metaphysician, his strongest influence thus far
has been upon theologians; but this fact is not surprising,
inasmuch as his philosophy has concentrated with amazing
single-mindedness upon the question of the nature and
reality of God. Moreover, two of Hartshorne's former stu-
dents, Schubert Ogden and John B. Cobb, Jr., are now
leading American theologians who are in the vanguard of
the most recent developments of that creative movement
known as "process theology." In general, American process
theology is consciously dependent upon the process philosophy of either Whitehead or Hartshorne or both; and
Hartshorne deserves a large amount of credit for doggedly
advocating Whiteheadian-Hartshornian process philosophy
during the past four decades when such advocacy was not
popular among either philosophers or theologians. After
being partially eclipsed for over two decades by Barthian,
Niebuhrian, or Tillichian theology, process theology of the
Whiteheadian-Hartshornian strand now stands forth in the
theological sunlight as one of the most creative and viable
options on the American scene. No one will be able to do
responsible theological work during the remainder of the
twentieth century without taking account of the philosophy

of Charles Hartshorne; and all who study it, layman and theologian alike, will be profited, if not fully convinced, by it.

Nevertheless, in addition to Hartshorne's influence on theology, his role in American philosophy has also been one of great significance. Along with Paul Weiss, he should probably be regarded as preeminent among living American philosophers who still pursue their work in the grand style of systematic metaphysical description and construction. For decades, Hartshorne and Weiss have tenaciously clung to their definite convictions that metaphysics is the main business of philosophy, despite almost overwhelming opposition from the powerful camps of American logical positivism, linguistic analysis, and their allies. Accordingly, Hartshorne's efforts to combine logical rigor with metaphysical description have been an enheartening example to many younger philosophers who have surmised that dogmatic exclusion of all metaphysical issues would eventually afflict philosophy with a fatal case of "analysis paralysis." Since the antimetaphysical ban has now been partially lifted by many philosophers, they are regarding Hartshorne's positions with increasing seriousness. Furthermore, in gratifying his metaphysical passion, Hartshorne has demonstrated that the deepest levels of metaphysics inevitably involve the question of God. This achievement alone is pregnant with enormous meaning and interest for philosophy and theology; and, in this regard, we must view Hartshorne as standing in the same tradition with Aristotle, Aquinas, Spinoza, Hegel, and Whitehead. Accordingly, philosophical thinkers everywhere may thank Hartshorne for his notable contributions in preserving and recovering a sense of the wholeness and grandeur of philosophy as the pursuit of that light and wisdom which alone can sustain civilized human life during a time when civilization seems gravely threatened.

In broad outline, Hartshorne's dependence upon Whitehead finds clearest expression in his enthusiastic adoption of Whitehead's view of the universe as essentially one of perpetual change and becoming. This view, which Hartshorne affirms without reservation, holds that everything, including God, is ceaselessly changing in a dynamic process of creative advance that will never end. Accordingly, the Whiteheadian-Hartshornian conception of the universe-in-process is squarely in opposition to the dominant views of traditional Western philosophy and theology. The traditional or classical vision of the universe has held that the basic realities of both God and the universe endure permanently without essential change. Hartshorne follows Whitehead in insisting that the only permanence anywhere occurs within and not above the ever-changing process. Both thinkers feel that one misconceives the nature of the entire universe as long as he fails to understand that becoming, dynamic, changing categories are more fundamental than being, static, and permanent categories.

Furthermore, Hartshorne fully shares Whitehead's idea that the ultimate components which constitute the universe are droplets of experience or feeling. These droplets are often called "actual entities" or "actual occasions," and they are not permanent things such as atoms but rather fleeting, transient events, occurrences, or happenings. Hartshorne claims that nature, man, and God are all composed of countless billions of these droplets of experience that occur and then pass away only to be succeeded by other similar events. Each such event is a type of experience that strives toward the realization of some value. In this manner, therefore, Hartshorne also adopts Whitehead's contention that the world is not a conglomeration of dead, material atoms but a vast congeries of fleeting aesthetic sensitivities or feelings. In other words, Whiteheadian-Hartshornian process philosophy maintains that every facet of the universe is alive, thus repudiating metaphysical materialism in all its forms.

A further feature of the Whiteheadian-Hartshornian vision of reality is its affirmation of the ultimate reality of the temporal process of creative advance. God becomes an indispensable aspect of the ever-advancing process and ceases to exist above or beyond the process in splendid isolation. Thus Hartshorne maintains that there is no eternity outside or above the temporal process. He asks man to live without eternity in any traditional sense and to be content with the everlastingness of temporal change. Of course, this view means that God is forever changing along with the world and that all divine, natural, and human life is properly oriented not to the past but to the future toward which all things ceaselessly move.

Although the subsequent chapters will develop these matters in detail, it might be helpful at this point to delineate briefly the main lines of development that Hartshorne has laid down for process theology. Of course, the various contemporary process theologians do not necessarily agree with Hartshorne in all details. However, such noteworthy process theologians as John B. Cobb, Jr., Schubert Ogden, W. Norman Pittenger, and Daniel Day Williams all acknowledge a profound debt to Hartshorne for assistance in carrying forward the theological task in a manner essentially dependent upon process philosophy. To say the least, Hartshorne's process philosophy has cogently stated some of the chief issues that process theologians are striving to resolve.

First and most strikingly, Hartshorne's philosophy radically reconceives the nature of God in order to obviate some notorious logical and moral difficulties in the traditional Western conception of God. His panentheistic doctrine of God* suggests that it is impossible to conceive of God apart from the world or the world apart from God. Hence, he discards the classical Christian doctrine of God's creation of the world out of nothing and affirms instead that the world, just as God, never had a real beginning and will never have a final end.

As one would expect, Hartshorne lays special stress on God's life as one of continual change and becoming instead of an unchanging life of eternal and static being. Hartshorne also abandons the notion of God's absolute and unchanging perfection and relates God's life and love crucially and decisively to the deeds of men and the events of the world. Moreover, Hartshorne contends that there is literally no end to God's everlastingly changing in response to perpetual changes in the cosmic process. Therefore, since God may always surpass himself and his previous perfections with every new experience, Hartshorne asserts that absolute perfection will never be attained even by God. An especially impressive facet of Hartshorne's vision of God is his relentless insistence that, in the midst of all God's joy and bliss, God also suffers most poignantly and excruciatingly as he witnesses the misery and tragedy of the creatures. By this means, Hartshorne has paved the way

---

* For a discussion and definition of this doctrine, see chapter 4.

for excitingly new possibilities for contemporary theological grappling with the age-old problem of evil.

In contrast to the views of the Barthian and biblical theologians, Hartshorne holds that the existence of God can be known and proved by means of human reason. He thus emphasizes that philosophy is indispensable for theology, tending to place much more stress upon sound philosophical reasoning than upon faithful acceptance of revelation. Consequently, process theologians in general regard philosophy as an essential ally in doing theology in a way that is incomprehensible to many theologians in conservative and neoorthodox camps.

Concordant with Hartshorne's tendency to minimize the importance of revelation as the basis for man's knowledge of God is his concern for a philosophy that places man in primary relationships to nature instead of to history. The chief emphasis, therefore, in much process theology is upon the need for satisfying modern man's quest for meaning and for making sense of his place in the cosmic universe. Likewise, there is a tendency among some (but not all) process theologians to neglect man's relation to history, including most importantly the salvation history witnessed to in the Bible. Among these process theologians, there is much more concern that their theology make some kind of sense to modern man than that it should be faithful to biblical revelation. Therefore, some process theologians are prepared to dispense partially or wholly with the idea that Jesus Christ is either the essential basis or central core of theology, although others would regard this mood as a tendency of process theology that needs drastic modification. In addition, process theology generally tends to follow

Hartshorne in neglecting or minimizing the ideas of man's sin and guilt and consequent need for atonement and repentance, ideas that have been central in many theological perspectives.

Another characteristic aspect that process theology derives from Hartshorne is its decisive rejection of humanism as a satisfactory option for modern man. Hartshorne grounds all of reality and all meaningful human existence directly upon God. It is because of this feature that process theology constitutes a vigorous challenge and a viable alternative to the paradoxical views of the "God-is-dead" theologians. The "God-is-dead" theology has suggested that all talk about God should be abandoned because it is meaningless to modern man. However, virtually the entire platform of the death-of-God theology has been effectively rejected by process theology, primarily because Whitehead and Hartshorne have marked out a path that enables the process theologians to understand how it still might be possible and necessary for man to speak meaningfully about God. This stance of process theology in opposition to theological humanism might well prove to be its historically most significant feature.

Hartshorne's treatment of the question of human immortality has also left its mark upon process theology. Because he doubts that there is any continuation of personal human experiences after death, he forcefully challenges all the traditional notions of life after death, including the doctrines of heaven and hell. Hartshorne's view of immortality is neither the humanistic one of immortality through posterity nor the Greek one of an immortal soul nor the biblical one of bodily resurrection but a very special one of being eternally remembered in the mind of God. This view stresses the unique, once-for-all, everlastingly significant meaning of this present human life. It thus accords well with the emphasis of process and other types of contemporary theology on what John Baillie called "the proper claims of earth." Process theology is emphatically positive in its evaluation of the character and importance of this present human life. It joins cause with the contemporary theologies that celebrate the possibilities and achievements of man's total secular life and that abominate a narrow religious isolationism. Consequently, process theology is helping to pave the way into new and still largely unexplored realms of interpretation of the nature of man's ethical life under God in this present world.

II. What is Really Real?

"... the social point of view is the final
point of view. All creatures are fellow creatures.
Nothing is wholly alien to us or devoid of inner
satisfactions with which, if we could grasp them,
we might more or less sympathize. It is merely a
question of how accessible to our perception and
understanding the inner values may be."
                                    —*The Logic of Perfection.*

THE CENTRALITY OF METAPHYSICS IN
HARTSHORNE'S PHILOSOPHY

All thinking persons assume that they know, at least in
part, what is really real. Many also know that at times
they have been deceived or mistaken in thinking that such
entities as pink elephants, dream images, or oases in
deserts were really "there" in the world when in actuality
they were not. Nevertheless, most people still believe that
they know the difference between realities and illusions,
mere wishes and hard facts, imaginary entities and actual
things. Moreover, most contemporary Westerners would
include minds, bodies, atoms, bacteria, airplanes, and
mountains in the class of things which they know to be
real; but they may be uncertain about the status in reality
of God, mathematical entities, and logical concepts such as

"possibility." The typical Western man probably feels sure that angels, devils, and spirits do not exist in reality but only as figments in deluded imaginations, but he is not ashamed to admit that he does not yet know whether there are such entities as people on other planets.

Nevertheless, the layman's common-sense view of reality is baffled by such conundrums as the nature of time and space, the reality of human freedom, quantum jumps in physics, or the claim of modern science that colors are not really present in the objects of perception but only in the mind of the beholder. In addition, when exposed to such hoary doctrines of some classical Eastern religions and philosophies as that of the fundamental unreality or illusory character of the entire material world and that of the all-encompassing reality of God, the average Westerner can only respond with astonishment and incredulity. When subjected to puzzles, paradoxes, or conflicts, the certitudes about reality of the philosophically unsophisticated man quickly become either dogmatisms, doubts, or confusions.

Obviously, no thoughtful person can escape at least some unsophisticated ventures into metaphysics, for "metaphysics" is what philosophers call the discussion about reality and unreality, being and nonbeing, or existence and nonexistence. "Metaphysics" as a term is derived from two Greek words which, when literally translated, mean "after physics"; but this translation is misleading, because proper metaphysics in philosophy *includes* (not follows) the entities known to physics within its total purview. True, metaphysics may pursue methods and descry entities beyond the scope of physics and the other sciences, but it intends to encompass rather than exclude authentic scientific methods and knowledge.

In a word, then, one's metaphysics is his comprehensive view of the universe or reality. A fully elaborated metaphysics would include an inventory of all real entities, a description of the various levels or degrees of reality or being, and an explanation of the nature of the difference between something and nothing or being and nonbeing. Customarily, philosophers will, for the sake of convenience, divide the metaphysical branch of philosophy into four major, interrelated subdivisions: ontology ("theory of being"), cosmology ("theory of the universe or nature"), anthropology ("theory of man"), and theology ("theory of God"). It seems, moreover, that the most satisfactory philosophy for the masses of mankind will be the one that affords the most adequate, comprehensive, and convincing answers to these four fundamental questions concerning the ultimate characteristics of being, nature, man, and God. And now to get to the point of this discussion, Charles Hartshorne is both willing and eager for his philosophy to be judged by this criterion.

As suggested in chapter one, Hartshorne has, in an era of widespread distrust or hostility on the part of philosophers toward metaphysics, remained unabashed in his commitment to metaphysics as the central concern of philosophy. Without disparaging the importance or intrinsic interest of such other philosophical disciplines as logic, theory of knowledge, or analysis of language, he has insisted that the urgent issues raised by these and other branches of philosophy can be viewed in proper perspective only within the context of an all-comprehensive metaphysical vision. And what an ambitiously all-encompassing metaphysical vision does Hartshorne delineate! Confident that metaphysics is a completely legitimate rational enterprise for philosophy, he avows that it studies that "logical class of entities, the universal categories of all actual and conceivable worlds." [1] Elsewhere, Hartshorne declares that his approach to metaphysics achieves "validity in principle for all cosmic epochs," [2] meaning that the metaphysical categories which he derives are applicable not only to all aspects of this immense universe but also to all facets of every possible future universe. Indeed the correct derivation of such categories would appear to be no mean achievement for the finite human reason.

Regarding the metaphysical enterprise, Hartshorne is in complete agreement with Whitehead's famous description of speculative philosophy:

> Speculative Philosophy is the endeavour to frame a coherent, logical, necessary system of general ideas in terms of which every element of our experience can be interpreted. By this notion of 'interpretation' I mean that everything of which we are conscious, as enjoyed, perceived, willed, or thought, shall have the character of a particular instance of the general scheme. Thus the philosophical scheme should be coherent, logical, and, in respect to its interpretation, applicable and adequate. Here 'applicable' means that some items of experience are thus interpretable, and 'adequate' means that there are no items incapable of such interpretation. [3]

Accordingly, Hartshorne defines metaphysics as "the search for necessary and categorial truth" and describes metaphysical truths as those which no experience can contradict and which any experience must illustrate. [4] In a helpful article on this subject, Hartshorne elaborates: "Metaphysics, in an old phrase, explores 'being *qua* being,' or reality *qua* reality, meaning by this, the strictly univer-

sal features of existential possibility, those which cannot
be unexemplified"; and he gives as an example of such
a necessary truth the affirmation that "experience as creative process occurs." [5]

Moreover, Hartshorne's optimism and his aesthetic passion are voiced in his declaration that the truth which
metaphysics discloses is both good and beautiful and that
it can never be evil or ugly or objectionable.[6] In tones
reminiscent of Plato, he affirms, "Metaphysical truth is in
some fashion a *realm of beauty unsullied by any hint of
ugliness.*" [7] Therefore, we may summarize his position by
stating that metaphysical inquiry for him is reason's
search for those contemplatively satisfying and beautiful
truths that are necessarily exemplified in all possible experiences and aspects of every possible or actual universe.

HARTSHORNE'S METHOD IN METAPHYSICS

Granted the legitimacy and desirability of Hartshorne's
conception of the quest for metaphysical truths, the crucial
question becomes *how* such a quest may be validly con-
ducted. But on this question of the proper method in
metaphysical research Hartshorne is quite explicit. A
lengthy quotation seems justified at this point as the best
means of setting forth his position:

> Metaphysics is not a deduction of consequences either from
> axioms dogmatically proclaimed true nor yet from mere
> arbitrary postulates or hypotheses. It is an attempt to describe
> the most general aspects of experience, to abstract from all
> that is special in our awareness, and to report as clearly and
> accurately as possible upon the residuum. In this process
> deduction from defined premises plays a role, but not the

role of expanding the implications of the axioms. The great historical error was to suppose that some metaphysical propositions have only to be announced to be seen true, and hence all their implications must be beyond questioning. The true role of deduction in metaphysics is not to bring out the content of the initially certain, but to bring out the meaning of tentative descriptions of the metaphysically ultimate in experience so that we shall be better able to judge if they do genuinely describe this ultimate. Axioms are not accepted as self-evident, then used to elicit consequences that must not be doubted. They are rather set up as *questions* whose full meaning only deduction of the consequences of possible answers can tell us.

When we know the meaning of the possible answers, we may, if we are lucky, be able to see that one of them is evidently true to that residuum of experience which is left when all details variable in imagination have been set aside. Thus, self-evidence or axiomatic status is the goal of the inquiry, not its starting point. Metaphysical deduction justifies its premises by the descriptive adequacy of its conclusions; it does not prove the conclusions by assuming the premises. In this, metaphysics is like inductive science.[8]

From this statement we learn that Hartshorne's method in metaphysics is one of *abstraction and descriptive generalization.* Since metaphysical truths are exemplified in all human experiences, they are exemplified in every one of our own concrete experiences. Therefore, if we could abstract those most general and common features of human experience from the welter of their vastly varied details, the residuum thus obtained would be metaphysical truth or truths; and, if our process of abstraction were sufficiently thorough and accurate, the resultant truths could be generalized as applying to all experiences in all possible universes. This statement of procedure makes manifest

Hartshorne's assumption that the microcosm of any particular human experience, at the utmost level of metaphysical generality, resembles the macrocosmic universe even though the latter is an almost infinitely vast conglomeration of other experiences.

If this assumption is allowed Hartshorne (and its denial would entail the undesirable conclusion that the universe is incorrigibly unknowable by man), then it is theoretically possible to sit in one's armchair and, by the method of abstraction and descriptive generalization, reflect one's way to the ultimate truths about all facets of the universe in this and every cosmic epoch! However, Hartshorne does provide for the testing of the process of metaphysical abstraction by an assessment of the descriptive adequacy of its resultant truths to other experiences than those from which the truths were originally abstracted. Moreover, he would be quick to acknowledge that the most frequent and fertile source of error in a metaphysics that follows his method would be the inevitable human limitations upon the metaphysician's powers to abstract from his experiences with *sufficient* generality for his conclusions to be universally valid. Finality and complete adequacy in metaphysical statement, manifestly, will never be achieved by man; and Hartshorne does not lay claim to these characteristics as properties of his own metaphysics. Yet he does contend that partial adequacy is possible and that he can demonstrate the necessity of some interesting and satisfying metaphysical truths—truths that are also vital to the peace and well-being of the human race. What these truths and their implications are the remainder of this book will seek to describe and assess.

THE ULTIMATE UNITS OF REALITY

Following the fashion set by the traditional founder of modern philosophy, René Descartes, Hartshorne locates the ground of metaphysical certainty in the immediate awareness of human consciousness. He reasons that the most certain and reliable knowledge accessible to man is the direct and intuitively self-evident knowledge of his own subjective experience. Since introspection gives us privileged access into the inner workings of our own consciousnesses, Hartshorne argues that, if we cannot have sure knowledge of human consciousness, then we cannot know anything else to which privileged access is not available; and his trust in reason will not permit him to acquiesce in the skeptical suggestion that no reliable knowledge is possible for man. Hence, the Hartshornian metaphysical edifice is based upon the bedrock of the fleeting human consciousness as the foundation and model of metaphysical knowledge. To Hartshorne it seems perfectly natural and obvious that subjective human awareness should be taken by all men as the ultimate clue to the nature of the universe:

> The human specious present is the only epoch we directly experience with any vividness, just as the spatial spread of a human experience is the only atomic unit. In perceiving the non-human world we are always apprehending collectives, both spatial and temporal. To form even a vague conception of the singulars composing these collectives our only resource is to generalize analogically the epochal and atomic characters of human experiences.[9]

On the basis, therefore, of the metaphysical clue to

reality discovered in human consciousness, Hartshorne deduces that the ultimate units of reality are the "atomic characters" of various experiences, which are varyingly designated as "unit-experiences," "experient-occasions," or "actual entities." [10] Here he is adopting Whitehead's succinctly-stated cosmology:

> 'Actual entities'—also termed 'actual occasions'—are the final real things of which the world is made up. There is no going behind actual entities to find anything more real. They differ among themselves: God is an actual entity, and so is the most trivial puff of existence in far-off empty space. But, though there are gradations of importance, and diversities of function, yet in the principles which actuality exemplifies all are on the same level. The final facts are, all alike, actual entities; and these actual entities are drops of experience, complex and interdependent.[11]

As will be explained in chapter four, Hartshorne disagrees with Whitehead's statement in this quotation that God is an actual entity; but, otherwise, Hartshorne's metaphysics totally agrees with Whitehead's declaration that the "final facts" are "actual entities" or "drops of experience." Moreover, each human being must be constituted of many millions of these "unit-happenings" or "experiences," because Hartshorne affirms that persons have about ten new ones per second and that they fit together so smoothly that the transitions between them go largely unnoticed.[12] And inasmuch as everything in the universe is composed of similar unit-experiences or actual entities, the number of them that occurs at any given instant of time (if we may legitimately speak of such instants) must be stupendously large. These myriads of drops of experience in the Whiteheadian-Hartshornian metaphysical

scheme correspond roughly to the monads of Leibniz's
world-view and to the energy quanta of modern physics as
the basic building blocks of the universe.

It is essential to understand that, according to Hartshorne, these drops of experience, as the ultimately real
entities, are not permanently enduring "things" but rather
very transient occurrences, happenings, occasions, acts, or
events. Moreover, all these events are thoroughly value-
oriented, for each one is a striving toward the realization
of some value. As Hartshorne says, "Experience is an act;
and every act at least strives to realize a value." [13] Therefore, the cosmic universe at any given moment is a vast
swarm of experience-events that are coming into existence, achieving some value, and passing out of existence.
Once an experience achieves its aim or realizes some
value, then it ceases to exist ("perishes" is Whitehead's
somewhat misleading term) in its unique form. Hartshorne insists that the values in question here are not ethical
values, since, according to him, ethical values cannot be
universal. Instead, he holds that these are aesthetic values
which are universal in scope. Hence, he concludes that
aesthetic values are immediate values that are present in
all experiences.[14]

Hartshorne is aware that his kind of metaphysics is a
revolutionary change in perspective for most people.
Whereas we usually think of things or people as individuals to which events happen, he advocates the converse
proposition that things or persons are "certain stabilities
. . . in the flux of events." [15] He claims the support of
modern science, especially current physics, for this recom-
mended reversal of cosmological outlook. For example,
he points out that quantum mechanics now suggests that

atoms are not moving entities or things *to which* events happen but rather *are* the sequences of events or happenings themselves. If this suggestion is accepted, then we must accustom ourselves to thinking that there really are no such things as particles, atomic or otherwise, but only "particle-like events." [16] Furthermore, when one becomes persuaded that such reasoning is sound and thus abandons the habit of supposing that events must happen *to* something rather than that happenings are the only real somethings, then he is well on the way toward a thoroughgoing Hartshornian cosmology.

In his first book, entitled *The Philosophy and Psychology of Sensation*, Hartshorne announces his agreement with the Whiteheadian idea that the materials of all nature are "events composed of aesthetic feeling," claiming the additional support of modern physics for the contention; and he has never wavered in this conviction. [17] Moreover, he also expounds in this work the further Whiteheadian notion, which he tirelessly repeats in his later works, that what the constituent experiences or feelings of the universe experience are *other* experiences. Hartshorne considers it obvious that no feeling can merely feel itself but must always feel other feelings, a doctrine which he says C. S. Peirce was among the first to hold. [18] Hence, he declares, "The world may be conceived as the increasing specification of the theme 'feeling of feeling' "; and he affirms that the "spontaneous conviction of all exalted moments of life" is the presentiment that the key to the nature of things is "the sensitiveness of living beings for each other." [19]

Accordingly, Hartshorne's main thesis in this book on sensation is that such occurrences as the human awareness of the color red are best explained as the results of an "affective continuum" in which the mind feels the redness of the brain cells (!) which feel the redness of light rays which in turn feel the redness of the object perceived.[20] Indeed, the conclusion of this work is adequately descriptive of Hartshorne's lifetime of metaphysical labors, so that a lengthy quotation may be justified:

> The possibility of a single science of nature at once follows. All individuals become comparable to ourselves, and physics may prove to be nothing but the behavioristic side of the psychology or sociology of the most universally distributed and low-grade or simple individuals. This is the only conception that can even pretend to represent an absolute ideal of scientific success. Its advantage is unique, and with every advance of science can only become more apparent. For everything moves toward it—at least in the sense that it brings us nearer to the completion of less ambitious programs, and hence to the time when they can no longer function as goals—and nothing can carry us beyond it. . . .
>
> The reason this ultimate program seems so remote or incredible is partly that we have as yet no real conception of the variables exhibited in human experience, and hence do not see how widely different values from any occurring in our experience are abstractly conceivable as missing areas or extended portions of the domains of potential characters which the variables permit. The reason is also partly our ignorance of the details of nature on its behavioristic side, the superficiality of even our physics and, much more, of our biology and physiology.
>
> When science has gained a more perfect picture of the spatio-temporal patterns exhibited by the life and adventures of a particle, including perhaps the evolution of the cosmos from a stage in which it did not contain this particle, and into one in which it will no longer contain it, then perhaps speculation as to an inner life of the particle, its pleasures, dis-

pleasures, etc., will take a more definite form. All science
may thus become natural history, and all individuals studied
by science, fellow-creatures. Physics will be but the most
primitive branch of comparative psychology or of general
sociology.[21]

We turn next to an explication of the term "panpsychism" as Hartshorne employs it.

PANPSYCHISM

Hartshorne defines "panpsychism" (from Greek words
meaning "all-soul") as "the view that all things, in all
their aspects, consist exclusively of 'souls,' that is, of various kinds of subjects, or units of experiencing, with their
qualifications, relations, and groupings, or communities." [22]
He acknowledges that the term is somewhat misleading,
because the ultimate unit-experiences are not the same as
the traditional concept of the human soul; but he is content to employ it because of some analogy of feeling-
experience between human souls and the actual entities.
Hartshornian panpsychism, then, realizes that there might
be infinitely many different kinds of "souls," ranging from
electrons to God, and, therefore, recommends that we
generalize our own internal experience as a cautiously
employed "infinitely flexible analogy."[23] It would set no
limits to the possible variety of psychic life, leaving to the
science of comparative psychology the task of actually describing the various kinds of souls there are; but it does
contend that all things, including ultramicroscopic entities,
consist of "minds" or "souls" even if many of them are
on an extremely low, subhuman level.[24] Hartshorne avows
that we are chiefly indebted to three great philosophers,

Plato, Leibniz, and Whitehead, for the creative insights that have brought panpsychism to its present impressive status as a full-scale metaphysical system.

Most obviously, Hartshorne's panpsychism should be understood paramountly as an explicit repudiation of metaphysical materialism in all its forms, both ancient and modern. Similarly, it also repudiates metaphysical dualism in Cartesian or other forms that maintain that both mind *and matter* are equally ultimate principles of reality. Hartshorne vigorously argues that there is no evidence whatsoever, whether scientific or metaphysical, that even unambiguously suggests that the ultimate atomic units of the universe are dead, inert, and unconscious. To be sure, his panpsychism holds that the ultimate constituent units of all things are atomic; but they are atoms of conscious "experience" at least remotely resembling human mental experiences. Hence, panpsychism categorically rejects as a colossal metaphysical error the entire tradition of atomistic materialism from Democritus to Lucretius to classical Newtonian mechanics.

Furthermore, Hartshorne launches a surprisingly strong assault upon the reigning scientific materialism of today and simultaneously presents a stout defense of his own position. For example, he asserts in the following fashion that there is not one shred of evidence that shows that the atomic and subatomic particles of physics must be lifeless or unconscious: "It is impossible to mention, and no one has mentioned, any fact which physics now asserts about the pattern of individual occurrences which contradicts the supposition that individuals as such are sentient creatures." [25] In other words, the assumption that modern science has revealed or demonstrated that the universe is

fundamentally composed of dead or mindless matter in
purely mechanical motion is completely unwarranted and
gratuitous.

Consequently, Hartshorne rejects the fashionable assumption that mind on planet earth has emerged from
what was once *mere* matter. He denies that the notion of
mere matter can be given any intelligible meaning, holding
that "mere matter" is a totally opaque concept. He also
disallows Descartes' suggestion that "extension" is the main
criterion of difference between matter and mind on the
grounds that it has not been shown that mind cannot be
extended in some respects. In addition, he contends that,
before one can talk meaningfully of a material stuff devoid
of experience, he must first show how to falsify the panpsychistic thesis that "mind or experience in some form
is everywhere"; but this prerequisite demonstration is theoretically impossible for finite minds, because experience
is conceivably capable of an infinity of forms and degrees. Therefore, he believes that he has a logically im-
pregnable position in affirming that the zero case of mind
would also be the zero case of reality.[26] Hence, either we
must talk about matter in terms of the infinitely flexible
"psychic variables" of human mental experience, or we
cannot talk intelligibly about it at all.[27] Thus Hartshorne
feels justified in the following caustic comment upon Santayana's defense of materialism: " 'Matter' is the asylum
of ignorance, pure and simple, whose only useful function
is to postpone for a more convenient occasion the specification of the type of psychic reality required in the given
case." [28]

Hartshorne does admit that panpsychism appears in-
credible to common sense at such points as the suggestion

that stones may have feelings or be composed of sentient entities; but he counters the force of this objection by pointing out that such scientific conceptions as atomic and cellular structures of plants and animals also greatly transcend common sense. He also grants the common-sense view that a human corpse is a dead thing as a human body, but he still makes his panpsychistic point by insisting that even a corpse is composed of many living things and, as far as our knowledge runs, nothing else.[29] In addition, he claims that his belief that there is only a relative and not an absolute distinction between mind and matter is given support by recent developments in physics that have shown that the differences between matter and various kinds of radiation are differences of degree and not of kind. Lest he be misunderstood, he says that panpsychism does not for once question the real existence of such entities as atoms or electrons but merely insists that such individuals must "feel" and "will." He does not shrink from the view that electrons "enjoy" their existence and deliberately alter their orbits in order to obtain vivid contrasts and thus avoid being bored.[30]

It is quite important to understand that, although Hartshorne's panpsychism resembles classical philosophical idealism in holding that reality is essentially mental or spiritual in character, it also defends the opposite of the standard Berkeleyan (or Kantian) idealism in epistemology or theory of knowledge. Whereas Berkeley seems to have maintained that an object is constituted by being known, Hartshorne's realistic position in epistemology explicitly states that an object of knowledge is entirely independent of its being known by any *particular* subject. Conversely, Hartshorne also affirms that the subject of any knowledge always depends upon the objects of which it is aware. The subject is a different subject for knowing a particular object, but that object is in no degree different for being known by that subject.

Moreover, Hartshorne affirms that he does not contradict himself when he asserts the additional twin theses that every concrete entity is a subject (or has objects of knowledge) and that every such entity must be an object for some (anyone will do) subject.[31] Furthermore, he argues that only the panpsychistic doctrine of an ocean of subjects internally related to their objects of knowledge can make sense of our deeply ingrained conception of the world as a real nexus of temporal succession of cause-effect relationships. Therefore, after extensive analysis of the many issues involved, he concludes emphatically that "we know nothing of a form of concreteness other than that of subjects" and that the only alternatives in ontology and cosmology are either panpsychism or agnosticism.[32]

SOCIAL PROCESS

It is now possible to understand why Hartshorne designates his ontology and cosmology as "societal realism," "social organicism," or "social process." He means that ultimate reality actually is one vast social process or complexity of myriads of social processes. Each of the quadrillions of experience-occasions that comprise the universe is immediately and intrinsically social in nature, for experience is always experience *of* something else, namely, other experiences ("feeling of feelings"). Accordingly, "sympathy" is a key category of Hartshorne's metaphysics. Every actual occasion "has intrinsic reference . . . to preceding occasions, with which it has some degree of sympathetic participation, echoing their qualities, but with a new overall quality of its own as it reacts to them." [33] That is, there are no completely isolated individuals in the universe. Every one of the ultimate units in the cosmos is related by some degree of awareness to some other ultimate events and responds sympathetically to this awareness. Preceding occasions act causally upon subsequent occasions, and the subsequent occasions react sympathetically to the preceding ones. The entire universe, therefore, may be envisioned as a virtually infinite series of instantaneous throbs and pulsations of sympathy. Moreover, all the larger (or more abstract) entities which are composed of the experience-events, from electrons to stones to animals to people to God, are bound in the bonds (or enjoy the freedom and love) of the universal sympathy.

We may now proceed to the exposition of Hartshorne's conception of "organism" and "society," which are for him intimately interrelated terms. He defines an "organism" as "a whole whose parts serve as 'organs' or instrument [sic] to purposes or end-values inherent in the whole." [34] For example, a man is aware of himself as an organism, since he is conscious of realizing purposes through the parts of his body as organs. Moreover, Hartshorne maintains that an organism may have other organisms as parts or organs but that not all the parts of organisms need themselves be organisms. The human being is the best example of this principle. A man is an organism composed of bodily cells which are likewise organisms; but a finger of his hand is an organ and not an organism, although it is composed of organisms (the cells) and is also part of the larger organism, the entire body.[35]

In addition, Hartshorne holds that every lesser organ and organism is "organic" in the sense of being parts of the one supreme cosmic organism, the universe, which he regards as a well-unified, purposive whole. Thus he can say that a mountain (or sandpile) is not itself an organism, being only an aggregation of molecules or atoms (or grains of sand); but a mountain is composed of organisms, the atoms or molecules, and is also an organic part of the cosmic organism. Such entities as plants and termite colonies Hartshorne designates as "quasi-organisms." They are composed of organisms, either plant cells or termites; but, since such groupings of organisms probably have no unified purpose of their own, they should not be regarded as true organisms. He concludes: "Thus it is reasonable to deny that mountains, trees, or termite colonies enjoy feelings, but not so reasonable to deny that atoms, tree-cells, and termites enjoy them." [36] Similarly, Hartshorne suggests that various collections of people, such as races, classes, or nations, do not have a "group mind," even though they may occasionally act with some unitary purpose; therefore, they are not to be considered genuine organisms. He looks askance at the idea of "any group mind above the human individual and below the mind of the entire cosmos." [37]

In order to forestall objections to his social-organic theory, Hartshorne states that an electron or some similar ultimate particle may still be an organism even though it has no parts. In such cases of the simplest organisms, they may respond sympathetically to (or feel) their nearest equal neighbors in a community-like relationship. Such simplest particles would resemble disembodied spirits because their only embodiment would be their environment.[38]

Hartshorne furnishes a similarly interesting reply to the converse objection that the entire universe could not be one organism, since it has no environment ("There is nowhere to go from the universe").[39] His neat reply to this difficulty is that, although the universe has no neighbors to which it may respond, it may still respond to its own "internal environment" or the various internal organs of which it is composed. The cosmic mind would, therefore, be the most fully embodied of all things, having the universe for its body, and would also be the integration of all lesser purposes, since its purpose would be the prosperity of all its parts and their collective totality.[40]

A further significant facet of Hartshorne's social conception of the universe is his idea that the wills or minds of organisms influence their component organs or parts as well as being influenced by them. For instance, he contends that the laws of quantum mechanics are not sufficient to account for all aspects of why human beings think as they do. His reason is that the electrons in the human brain are not only influenced in their actions by other electrons but also by the fact that they are parts of a human brain and thus must move in certain ways partly because the human being thinks as he does.[41] Nevertheless, Hartshorne also affirms that no organism may completely control or dominate its constituent parts. Moreover, he regards this as a self-evident truth, since total domination of the part by the whole would erase all meaningful distinctions between them. Furthermore, if one keeps clearly in mind the all-important time factor of Hartshorne's societalism, it becomes clear that an actual whole can never act upon the actualities of which it is composed at any given moment but only upon *subsequent* actualities.

Hartshorne suggests that organisms may helpfully be regarded as societies which fall into two broadly different types, "democracies" and "monarchies." The democratic societies have no one supreme or dominant member, with examples being such things possibly as stones and probably as some cell-colonies and even special forms of many-celled plants and animals.[42] Monarchic societies, on the other hand, do have a supreme or dominant member which radically subordinates the parts to its ruling purpose but which can never completely rob the parts of all measure of control over themselves. The best example of the monarchic society seems to be the case of the human personality which controls (albeit only partially) its own bodily cells. The human personality also presents the fascinating case of a monarchic society that may have democratic societies among its constituents; e.g., the cells of the heart appear to have no dominant member, although the total personality may influence the heart's action to a certain extent. Hartshorne finds in this particular case a suggestive analogy for understanding the cosmic organism. The suggestion is that all societies, including the most democratic ones, are parts of an all-inclusive monarchic society, namely, the whole universe which is ordered by a single ruling member.[43] Little examination is required to discern that the single ruling member of the universal organism or society is what Hartshorne understands God to be. The full explication of his doctrine of God, however, will be reserved for a later chapter.

UNIVERSAL BECOMING

As previously indicated, Hartshorne's metaphysics draws

very heavily upon Whitehead's insights, and Hartshorne justifiably looks upon their common version of process philosophy as presenting a profound shift of perspective in Western metaphysics. He deliberately sets his "neoclassical metaphysics" in opposition and contrast to the heretofore dominant "classical" metaphysics of Western philosophy. One of the major differences between the two rival systems revolves around the terms "being" and "becoming." For classical Western metaphysics, such categories as "being" and "substance" are the more fundamental concepts, and "becoming" and "change" are explained in terms of being. The Whiteheadian-Hartshornian neoclassical metaphysics takes precisely the opposite tack: it treats "becoming" and "change" as the absolutely fundamental categories and accounts for "being" as an aspect *of* or *within* becoming. According to Hartshorne, Western classical metaphysics, receiving a powerful impetus from the depreciation of change by Plato and Aristotle, reached its culmination in medieval theology. This theology denied any change or contingency in the world on the grounds that their possibility was logically excluded by the assertion that the omniscient and immutable God could not change in any of his aspects, including his knowledge.

In contrast, Hartshorne affirms that Buddhism, in Eastern philosophy, was the earliest great philosophy to stress becoming as basic reality. It insisted that momentary experiences which do not "change" but just "become" are the primary realities, a notion not fully developed in Western philosophy until Whitehead did so in the twentieth century.[44] This emphasis in Buddhism largely accounts for the fact that Hartshorne frequently alludes to,

and allies himself with, certain important features of
Buddhist religious philosophy.

As far as Hartshorne is concerned, all the efforts of
classical metaphysics down to the present day to explain
becoming in terms of being are bound to be dismal fail-
ures. Instead of "explaining" change, they all essentially
deny change by affirming that it is unreal or mere appear-
ance or "being" viewed from the finite human perspective.
And inasmuch as change is intuitively obvious to the universal common-sense experience of mankind, Hartshorne
reasons that a metaphysics which denies change deserves
universal rejection. Contrastingly, Hartshorne's neoclassical metaphysics claims to provide a fully adequate explanation of being and permanence in terms of becoming.
Succinctly stated, the explanation is as follows.

The ultimate units of experience, the actual occasions,
just "happen" by virtue of creating themselves. However,
in their self-creation, they always "remember" aspects of
the immediately preceding occasions while creating a new
synthesis of experience. Therefore, some facets of the past
are always preserved in each succeeding set of experient-
events, a process that literally goes on forever. It is the
preserved aspects of past experiences in the ever-renewing
present that we designate by such terms as "being," "substance," "permanence," and "stability." For example, the
permanence of human personality consists in certain remembered aspects of past experiences that may occur as
rapidly as ten per second. Hence, Hartshorne maintains
that neoclassical metaphysics does not at all deny being
and permanence but rather affirms them—as aspects
within the more ultimate process of universal and perpetual
becoming.

Obviously, process metaphysics is an excitingly different vision of an everlastingly dynamic reality in comparison with the static universe of classical metaphysics. The world of neoclassical metaphysics is a world that is fresh and new every moment; but, of course, it is not totally new, inasmuch as the perpetually new creative syntheses of each moment always utilize elements of the previous creations.[45] Hartshorne's own summary statement is appropriate: "Neoclassical metaphysics is the fusion of the idealism or panpsychicalism which is implicit or explicit in all metaphysics with the full realization of the primacy of becoming as self-creativity or creative synthesis, feeding only upon its own products forever." [46] Surely, some elements of Hartshorne's impressive statement of his vision of an awesomely dynamic universe deserve not to be forgotten but to be preserved in all serious future efforts to create new syntheses in metaphysics!

The issue concerning the nature of time is inextricably intertwined with the notions of being and becoming, and the Hartshornian solutions to the problem are, as usual, intriguing. Just as he repudiates all conceptions of being that make problematic the reality of becoming, so Hartshorne also scorns all versions of time and eternity that swallow up time in eternity. His own constructive statement of the relationship may be described as an engulfing of eternity by the temporal process that is everlasting in duration.

In this regard, Hartshorne's main strictures are directed against those theologians and metaphysicians who advance views that imply the eradication of all meaningful distinctions among past, present, and future times. Included in this group of thinkers would be all theologians who insist that the omniscient God knows in detail all future events from the beginning and all philosophers who (following Laplace) contend that the present state of matter in the universe has conclusively determined in detail all future states of the universe. Both approaches, according to Hartshorne, obliterate all real distinctions between present and future by implying that all events are real now in an eternal present that can be known by a properly qualified (i.e., omniscient) being. Such unwarranted "spatializations" (Bergson) of time thus make nonsense of the idea of genuinely creative becoming and, therefore, are contrary to man's intuitive experience.

In contrast to such views, Hartshorne explicitly negates the notion that the events of the future can be known in detail by *any* being, including God. His line of reasoning is that, until they actually occur, all future events and their alternatives are merely possible, not actual; and even an omniscient God cannot know as actual what in fact is not actual but only possible. God knows the actual as actual and the merely possible as merely possible. For example, God cannot know specifically how many people will be living on earth at midnight, January 1, 2000 A.D., for that number will not be precisely determined until that precise date. Consequently, no completely true statements can now be made about such future realities.

Just as he does with becoming, so Hartshorne affirms the ultimate reality of the temporal process. The only eternity there is, according to him, is not beyond but within that process. Describing his constructive theory as "modal-psychological," he takes some cues from St. Augustine and suggests that the temporal dimension of reality may be "best conceived as the memory-creativity structure of experience as such." [47] If we follow his suggestions, the relations of contemporary things should be conceived of in terms of mutual involvement or noninvolvement, the past should be viewed as the perpetual memory of all that has happened to become determinate and actual, and the future should be considered as the anticipation of possibilities that are not yet actual and determinate.[48]

For Hartshorne, obviously, there is a fundamental difference between the past and the future, the past being the realm of actual individualities and the future being the realm of potential or possible individualities.[49] Thus it is not inaccurate to say that the past is real in a way that the future is not. Hartshorne finds important evidence for this modal asymmetry between past and future in the human ability to remember past events vividly and in detail and to anticipate the future only vaguely and generally.[50] Moreover, he holds that the past is completely fixed in irrevocable detail, since every event, once it is actualized, is real forevermore. Once an individual becomes, he never "unbecomes," because something cannot ever literally become nothing in Hartshorne's cosmology. The reality of past events is partially preserved as newly synthesized elements in later events but fully and infallibly in the never-failing memory of God.[51] Hartshorne explains further that a denial of the full reality of the past would entail the conclusion that no true statements could be made about the determinate character of past events ("Lincoln was assassinated"), whereas acceptance of his doctrine of the nonactuality of the future entails the falsity of all statements that ascribe completely determinate character to future events.[52] "Maybe" is the *only* correct mode of reference to the future.

INEVITABLE FREEDOM AND TRAGEDY

An unusually striking and important feature of Hartshorne's cosmology is his oft-repeated insistence upon the
reality and universality of freedom in nature. The creative
aspect of becoming in his philosophy of process involves
the idea that freedom is of the very essence of reality.
Moreover, he believes that the question of real freedom,
especially for man, is not merely academic but of vital
practical concern to the future well-being of all humanity.
In his opinion, any metaphysics is dangerous if it mini-
mizes the possibility of radical evil through the misuse of
freedom. Evil and tragedy are both grimly possible and
actual if freedom is genuine. Accordingly, there is some
validity to pessimism as one contemplates the real capacity
of the human race to do evil and the possibility that mankind may precipitate incalculably tragic evil and suffering
by its wrong decisions regarding destructive warfare and
the population explosion.[53] Given creative becoming as an
everlastingly continuous process, Hartshorne declares that
there will always be some evil in the world; but the
amount of evil will always be at least partially determined
by creative choices. Indeed, he acknowledges that the universality of freedom means that there is an element of
stark tragedy inherent in the very constitution of the universe. Following Berdyaev, he traces the root of tragedy
to creative freedom and avows that mankind will always
be confronted with pervasive peril as well as sublime opportunity. He elaborates as follows:

> All free creatures are inevitably more or less dangerous to
> other creatures, and the most free creatures are the most
> dangerous. Optimistic notions of inevitable, and almost effort-

less, progress are oblivious to this truth. They have tended to
unfit us for our responsibilities. Man needs to know that he
is born to freedom, hence to tragedy, but also to opportunity.
He could be harmless enough, were he less free. Freedom is
our opportunity and our tragic destiny. To face this tragedy
courageously we need an adequate vision of the opportunity,
as well as of the danger.[54]

Hartshorne clearly realizes that the manner of his defense of genuine freedom necessitates a definite break with
metaphysical determinism in all its guises; and, consequently, he launches a vigorous attack upon it in several
of his works. By "determinism" he means the view which
asserts that all events are *totally* determined by their antecedent causes, so that, given a certain set of antecedent
conditions, a particular result *must* follow necessarily. In
contrast, he retorts that such complete determinism is
never true for *any* event. In order to prevent any miscon-
ception, he stresses that neoclassical metaphysics does not
contend that some events are uncaused but only that no
events are fully determined by their causes.[55] More fully,
Hartshorne holds that all events (or ultimate individuals)
have partial causes and no events have complete causes.
Thus, in an important essay, he argues that "freedom requires indeterminism and universal causality." [56] He freely
admits that there is an element of regularity and order in
nature which may be partially described in the statistical
laws of science; but he also confesses his inability to give
a rational explanation (other than the immanence of God)
of why, in a world of freedom, we have an orderly cosmos
instead of sheer chaos.[57]

Hartshorne's view is that, although antecedent circumstances may predetermine in general the character of the

next event, they cannot determine it absolutely and in all detail. Each moment exists in partial independence of all predecessors by virtue of an element of chance novelty and spontaneity in each occurrence; and this element of chance in each event means that it must be undeducible and un-predictable in determinate detail from all its predecessors combined.[58] Therefore, he reasons that nothing, not even God, can rob persons of the self-determination that achieves a new creative synthesis in each moment of experience.[59] In a brief paragraph, he delineates clearly the nature of freedom which is the birthright of every individual:

> Freedom is an indetermination in the potentialities for present action which are constituted by *all* the influences and stimuli, all "heredity and environment," all past experiences, an indetermination removed only by the actuality (event, experience, act) itself, and always in such fashion that other acts of determination would have been possible in view of the given total conditions up to the moment of the act. A free act is the resolution of an uncertainty inherent in the totality of the influences to which the act is subject. The conditions decide what can be done and cannot; but what is done is always more determinate than merely what can be done. The latter is a range of possibilities for action, not a particular act.[60]

Hartshorne's elaborate critique of determinism is too detailed and intricate to be adequately surveyed here, so that we shall have to be content with briefly stating only a few of many carefully wrought out points.[61] First, he calls attention to the fact that modern metaphysical determinism arose in the Newtonian era when it was believed that sci-ence discovers absolute and immutable natural laws, but science has now totally abandoned this conception of law in favor of the theory that scientific laws are merely statistical descriptions of the way nature *happens* to work. Second, there has never been scientifically discovered and demonstrated a single law that is absolutely valid for all times and circumstances. Next, recent developments in quantum physics have revealed an ineradicable indeterminacy concerning motions of electrons, and thus we *may* have a hint from physical science itself that there is some contingency in the ultimate physical particles. Fourth, man in moments of decision is intuitively aware of contingencies in his actual determinations of the future, for he often chooses from a continuum of infinitely varied possibilities. Fifth, determinism implies that the concept of possibility is vacuous and that time and change are essentially unreal; but Hartshorne contends that he can rationally demonstrate that all three of these concepts, taken in their most pregnant sense, are indispensable categories. In sum, then, there is something logically arbitrary about every detail of the universe which the determinist cannot eradicate. Indeed, Hartshorne goes as far as to say that "the world as a whole is a matter of chance." [62] In the final analysis, things happen just because they happen; there is no sufficient reason why things are as they are, and *"preference is ultimate."* [63]

What is really real? With remarkable tenacity and consistency, Hartshorne has expended his lifetime in teaching and writing that the only satisfying answer to this age-old query must come from man's direct interrogation of his most intimate experience, namely, his own intuitively discerned consciousness. From this source, if he has rightly divined the matter, disciplined rational insight may discern that the ultimate components of this actual universe

(and of every possible universe) must be evanescent occasions of sympathetic experience of other experiences
which create themselves in freedom and love and then
dissolve at once into new syntheses of experience in a
vast, dynamic process that shall never cease.

III. What Is Man?

"Things or persons can then be only certain stabilities or coherences in the flux of events. The
stabilities are in the events, not the events in the
stabilities."

—*The Logic of Perfection.*

As explained in chapter two, Hartshorne regards human
conscious experience as our only reliable key to unlock
the mysteries of reality. He is well aware that this procedure of taking human experience as the model of all
reality may provoke from some quarters the charge against
his metaphysics of unmitigated anthropomorphism. However, he denies the fairness and accuracy of this allega-
tion, contending that his method is the only way philosophy
can escape both radical skepticism about ultimate reality
and an unwarranted tendency to assume that all of nature
resembles human experience. He says that taking experience as the basic clue to reality enables the metaphysician to evade anthropomorphism because "experience" is
a category that is capable of unlimited expansion and
variation. Consequently, to say that nature ultimately
consists of experience does not at all imply that all these
experiences are necessarily human. Rather, it is to suggest that human experience is merely one point on a prac-
tically infinite continuum of experiences and that other

53

points on this fundamental cosmological continuum may
be almost infinitely different from the human in intensity
and quality of experience. To give one specific example,
it is surely impossible for us to conceive of what an electron's experience would be like, but we must conceive of it
as *some kind* of experience or not conceive of it at all.[1]
Therefore, it is probably less misleading to state that
human experience is the one keyhole through which man
may catch a fleeting glimpse of the vast panorama of the
universe instead of the clue that solves the riddles of the
cosmos. Hartshorne would be the first to acknowledge
that countless enigmas and puzzles will remain even after
the work of the most comprehensive and adequate metaphysical analysis has been done.

Nevertheless, it must also be said that, although Hartshorne has an understandable penchant for treating man
as a somewhat special case, he in no wise thinks of man as
an exception to his basic metaphysical vision that was
depicted in the preceding chapter. Hartshorne's view is
that man is our best-understood case of exemplification
of the basic metaphysical categories. In other words, his
anthropology should be interpreted merely as a special
instance within the broad context of his ontology, cosmology, and (as we shall see) theology. For this reason,
this chapter on Hartshorne's doctrine of man is located
most appropriately between the previous one on his ontology and cosmology and the next one on his doctrine
of God. For him, man should be comprehended within
a cosmic context, but neither man nor the cosmos can be
rationally understood apart from God.

Moreover, it does not seem unfair to say that the questions of nature and God have been Hartshorne's most

profound and direct philosophical concerns and that he illuminates the human scene chiefly by indirect light reflected from these other two primary focal points of his intellectual analysis.

PERSONAL IDENTITY

Perhaps the most startling feature to Western minds of Hartshorne's (and Whitehead's) philosophy is its conception of human personal identity. In this regard, Hartshorne remains fully consistent with the other principles of process philosophy and abandons entirely the "substance" theory of the human soul or self as held by Plato, Augustine, Kant and other classical Western metaphysicians. In the most *concrete* terms, according to Hartshorne, there is no permanently or continuously enduring human ego or soul or self. Therefore, he declares that human individuality and identity may not be properly defined in terms of a self-identical soul that persists unchanged from conception to death and perhaps beyond. To be sure, Hartshorne does not say that human identity through change is unreal or illusory, but he does assert that it is an *abstraction* and not a concrete entity. He means that, in regard to the question of absolute identity, an enduring human soul or ego may be abstractly real but may not be concretely real.

Then what *is* concretely real or actual about human personality? Precisely what is concrete reality about all things in the universe, namely, the "unit-experiences" or "experient-occasions" that are the fundamental components of the cosmos? To quote Hartshorne: "My life consists of hundreds of thousands of selves, if by self is

meant subjects with strict identity." [2] The "subjects with
strict identity" are, of course, the actual occasions of the
Hartshornian cosmology. In fact, if we agree with him
that human experiences of as brief a duration as one-tenth
of a second may be distinguished in consciousness, and
if we disregard the problem of whether a sleeping person
also experiences at about the same rate of ten occasions
per second, then simple arithmetic enables us to conclude
that the concrete reality of a human being that lives
seventy years is well over two billion individual "selves"!
In addition, this staggering sum is dwarfed by the countless trillions of events that constitute the electrons, atoms,
molecules, cells, and organs that comprise that complex
society of occasions that we call the body of a person who
lives to age seventy. Speaking concretely, Hartshorne says
that a man is a new self or person about every one-tenth
of a second.

Undoubtedly, Hartshorne's definition of a self as in
actuality billions of selves is startlingly paradoxical—
at least at first glance. However, he contends that he has
strong arguments in its favor, including the argument
that it is much more paradoxical to try to explain how a
self-identical human self could really change through the
various stages of development that a normal human life
undergoes. Another argument is that no human ego ever
knows itself to be the very same ego throughout a lifetime. Where is this ego when the person is asleep? And
in what sense does the living self in the concrete present
identify itself as the selfsame ego of the newborn infant
it once was or the senile octogenarian it might become?
Is not the truth that each individual self knows itself
as new each moment, remembering previous selves and

anticipating future selves that are distinctive occurrences in their own specious moment of existence? [3]

Another argument is simply that analysis shows the impossibility of a self-identical self's having a continuous series of new experiences without becoming a different self in the process. Each new experience, if added to the old self, would make that self a new totality that is different from the previous self by virtue of the newly added experience. Therefore, each moment of experience of the human self must make it a slightly different and novel self. The new self of each moment partly includes the old experiences through memory, although Hartshorne does not exclude as inappropriate some talk of an old self with new experiences, provided it is clearly understood that the old self is contained within the new experiences and not the converse.[4] Furthermore, he reasons that, if human experiences were the properties of an identical ego instead of the ego's being the property of the experiences, then to know an individual ego would mean to know all its future; and, therefore, we could not really know the individual in question until his death.[5]

As hinted in the previous paragraph, Hartshorne does not seek to proscribe all talk of personal identity, personality traits, and other enduring objects. His primary point is that the identity through change of such entities, though real enough on its own level, is something of an abstraction from its constituent concrete events. Moreover, he has recently conceded that a person, such as Charles Hartshorne, is "almost concrete," i.e., concrete by comparison with such more abstract entities as "triangle" or "being human." [6] For example, "Charles Hartshorne" is a great abstraction in comparison with the billions of events or selves that have constituted that one human life; but it is also pointedly concrete by contrast with the notion of "human being."

Succinctly stated, Hartshorne's position regarding the personal identity of man (or animals or what-have-you) is that a man *is* his experiences instead of *has* them. The experiences "have" the man or the personality. Thus a particular man is the common denominator of a connected series of experiences. "He" *is* the relatively abstract common feature of the sequence of states (or selves or experiences) that fit together in a succession that begins with conception and ends in death.[7] Moreover, the primary bond that binds these states together into a distinctive series is that of sympathetic feeling, of which the two chief expressions are memory and anticipation. Sympathetic memory and anticipation, which are ingredient in every occasion of experience, are the forces that give a measure of identity through change to the present actual experience and past and future experiences in the same sequence.[8]

Hartshorne is not oblivious to the fact that his (and Whitehead's) concept of human individuality poses some serious problems for our traditional concepts of personal responsibility and social justice, but he contends that the difficulties in question are not insurmountable. For example, he asserts that it is not a particular man or personality that performs a given deed but rather a momentary self or sequence of such selves. This means that one momentary self does a certain deed, and then another later momentary self in the same series may receive rewards or punishments for it. In fact, Hartshorne declares that the only reward a given momentary self can receive is the reward

given in and with its own momentary activity, for there-
after it has ceased to exist in its unique particularity.[9]

The relevance of this theory to current notions of guilt
and moral responsibility is patent. Should a court punish
a different, later self for what another, earlier self has
done? Also, should one self repent for the misdeeds of
a previous self? Undismayed by such conundrums, Hartshorne suggests a possibly affirmative answer to both questions. Since any later self, though new in some respects,
may also have a tendency to misbehavior similar to that
of a previous self, both punishment and repentance may
be in order for the purpose of achieving a relevant trans-
formation of character. But once a pertinent change of
character has been obtained, Hartshorne feels that further
punishment of a particular man is ethically unjustified—
even though it may have some political justification as
society's best means of appeasing the anger of those who
have been victimized by the "guilty party." [10]

MAN AS A PSYCHOPHYSICAL ORGANISM

Just as Hartshorne's cosmology abandons the traditional
Western metaphysical dualism of matter and mind, so his
anthropology rejects the derivative notion, explicitly ad-
vocated by Plato and Descartes, that man is basically a
dualistic being composed of a material body and a spiritual soul. Instead, he prefers to think of man as an
organism that has a "psychical" pole and a "physical" pole
that are mutually interactive and reciprocally dependent.
Naturally, he does not object to the use of such terminology as "body" and "soul," provided it is remembered
that the human body is essentially a vastly complex

society of actual occasions and the human soul is the unifying, purposive agency of the body. Occasionally, Hartshorne even speaks of a "besouled body," but by such language he means only the probability of certain modes of action and experience that embody a given personality's characteristic traits.[11] Consequently, he suggests that, when a person's body goes into a deep, dreamless sleep, the soul loses its actuality, only to regain it when the person awakens.[12] Understandably, therefore, he disregards as inapplicable to his own view Gilbert Ryle's well-known caricature of Cartesian anthropological dualism as "the dogma of the Ghost in the Machine" —especially since Hartshorne denies that the human body is a "machine" in any materialistic, mechanical sense.[13]

In more typically Hartshornian language, a human being is a complex unity of two distinguishable-but-mutually-interrelated sequences of actual events: the sequence of processes in his bodily cells ("body") and the sequence of distinctively human or personal experiences ("mind" or "soul"). Moreover, Hartshorne holds that the interrelationship between the human body and mind is so intimate and reciprocal that the term "psychophysical organism" seems to be the most accurate one for designating his total view of the person. As a result, it becomes apparent that Hartshorne's doctrine of man bears some important resemblance to modern psychosomatic theories of personality and to the wholistic views of man dominant in twentieth-century biblical theology.

Hartshorne is unwilling for man to be regarded simply as the cellular processes of his body. This unwillingness is based primarily upon what he considers to be an undeniable and irreducible fact of human self-intuition:

when one is directly aware of himself in a specific moment, he is aware of "himself" as a single unit of action and not of any system of cells. Therefore, Hartshorne reasons that man is more than his cellular processess and is as much a "single dynamic unit" as any of the electrons or cells that constitute his body.[14]

Furthermore, in the explication of his understanding of man, Hartshorne does not shrink from the somewhat novel and strange proposition that the human mind may possess properties that have traditionally been ascribed only to matter, namely, location and extension in space. He says that the human mind has a place or places in space in close proximity to the parts of the body and hence must also possess size, shape, and motion. The following sentence adequately expresses his position:

> It can be inferred with some probability that the human mind, at any given moment, is not drastically different in size and shape from the pattern of activity in the nervous system with which at that moment it interacts, and as this activity moves about somewhat it follows that the mind literally moves in brain and nerves, though in ways unimaginably various and intricate.[15]

Moreover, if it be objected that the human mind derives its spatial character from its association with the body, Hartshorne's rejoinder is that the converse proposition is equally true. That is, one could not know where his body is apart from his mind, for one locates his body always only in connection with the feeling or sensing of his mind.[16]

Concerning the manner of interaction between mind and body, Hartshorne maintains that there is only one possible intelligible explanation. It is that human mental experiences "immediately sympathize" with certain sub-human experiences of the cells in the body and that the converse relationship also holds to some extent. For example, the experience of suffering is, via sympathy, mutual between me and my cells. When they suffer, I suffer; and when I suffer, they suffer too.[17] Hartshorne further contends that this view of interaction as sympathy has the merit of accounting both for the dependence of the mind upon the states of the cells in the brain and nervous system and for the power of the mind to control, within certain limits, the cells of the body.[18] Given that the molecules and/or cells of the body have a certain amount of psychical life, continuous reciprocal interaction in the form of "organic sympathy" seems to be the only perfectly natural explanation for the obvious influence that body has upon mind and vice versa.[19]

In cases of human volition Hartshorne finds the clearest examples of the control of mind over body and, indeed, the only transparent instances of the direct control of one entity over another. In a typical instance of a person's volition regarding an overt bodily movement, Hartshorne says that the will or ego directly activates the nervous mechanism, which in turn directs the muscles, which eventually accomplish the desired movement. The important point is that the only relationship of power between the will and the nerves is one of organic sympathy. In his words, *"The immediate object of effective human volition is a change in the human body."* [20]

Furthermore, according to Hartshorne, the relationships involved in human knowledge by means of perception are analogous to those obtaining in cases of volition. He states that a man may have immediate awarenesses of two kinds: intuitive awareness of his own thoughts and feelings and sympathetic awareness of certain changes in parts of his body.[21] The second type of direct human awareness involves the principle that the objects immediately known in sensation or perception are always objects *inside* the body and never objects outside the body. In developing this principle, Hartshorne declares that no one can ever know any event outside his body with anything like the vividness and directness which may characterize his direct awareness of some bodily events.[22]

Beginning with his doctrine of the "affective continuum"[23] in *The Philosophy and Psychology of Sensation*, Hartshorne has taken pains to spell out some of the startling consequences of his view of sensation as outlined in the previous paragraph. In part, his idea is that sensation is always "representative" of objects outside the body but directly "presentative" of the actual states of cells within the body.[24] But now we come to the truly sensational aspect of his understanding of sensation! It is that "brain states flower into sensations" in such fashion that, when one senses certain qualities such as redness or sweetness or roundness associated with an object such as an apple, those perceived qualities are mainly the properties of his brain cells and not of the objects. Presumably, therefore, when one has the vivid perception of a hot stove associated with touching it, he is directly perceiving the "hotness" of his own bodily cells and only by indirection the hotness of the stove. Hartshorne intrepidly draws numerous conclusions of this sort, stoutly maintaining that his theory makes for more comprehensive sense than the traditional view that holds that, when one sees an external object, he really sees the object and not just a certain

shape in his own brain. Accordingly, he upholds the
"social-organic" view of sensation to the effect that the
body can never do other than "echo" or "represent" its
surroundings and directly "present" its own states to the
immediately sympathetic human awareness.[25]

If the human body and mind communicate directly
through reciprocal sympathy, how do human beings
communicate with each other? In the same way? "No,
fortunately," replies Hartshorne. If human beings could
communicate among themselves by direct sympathy, then
they would be as mutually dependent upon each other as
the body and mind are; and this condition would deny
individual persons freedom and distinct individuality over
against one another.[26] Although the relationship between
one's body and mind seems to be immediately social,
Hartshorne holds that interchange between human minds
is almost never by direct contact and generally through
mediation of vibrating particles of air and other kinds
of "matter." Therefore, individual human freedom, independence, and privacy are preserved, and still human
beings appear to be able to communicate meaningfully
and accurately with one another. According to Hartshorne,
that human bodily cells lack such freedom and privacy
with respect to the human mind should not be objectionable
to them because of their radically inferior status; but a
similar relationship of inferiority-superiority among human beings would be absolutely intolerable because it
would rob some of their humanity.[27]

HUMAN EXISTENCE AS SOCIALITY AND LOVE

As explained in chapter two and the preceding sections

of this chapter, Hartshorne's ultimate entities, the actual
occasions of experience, are all social by nature. Their
entire awareness is a sympathetic feeling of the feelings
of other entities. On the human level, the experient-
events of the body feel sympathy for other events in the
same sequence, and the same holds true for the events
in the same mental sequence. Moreover, the individual's
bodily cells have direct sympathy for his mind, and vice
versa. Furthermore, Hartshorne asserts that human beings
should have a measure of mediated and rationally based
sympathy for all other human beings and, indeed, for all
things in the universe.

Hartshorne beautifully defines "social" as the coordi-
nate processes of weaving one's own life from strands
taken from the lives of others and giving one's own life
as a strand to be woven into their lives.[28] He also defines
"self-interest" as the sympathy the present self may feel
for future members of the *same* sequence, and "altruism"
as "whatever sympathy that self may feel for members
of other sequences, human, sub-human, or superhuman." [29]
In addition, he suggests that every momentary self is
really altruistic because of its innate interest in other
selves and thus that "self-interest" is actually a special
case within this universal altruism at the level of the
ultimately concrete entities.[30]

Furthermore, Hartshorne affirms his faith that human
beings are often motivated by genuinely altruistic desires
which are not merely forms of disguised self-interest. For
instance, one may plan sympathetically for the welfare
of others long after his death through such actions as
making a will or buying life insurance, and he may enjoy
these actions; but he does them not just for his own en-

joyment but also for the future recipients of the blessings
of his benevolence.[31] However, Hartshorne maintains that
such universally common altruistic actions can only be
fully comprehended rationally by appeal to God as superhuman mind who ultimately unites all persons and
entities in his infinite awareness and memory. On this
level, therefore, as well as on many others, as far as
Hartshorne is concerned, the analysis of man "drives on"
(Tillich) to the question of God.[32] Moreover, once one
attains the vision of all things as united in the mind of
God, he has reached the ultimate Hartshornian rational
basis for feeling sympathetic respect for all creatures as
contributing to the life of God. However, this reasoning
does not lead Hartshorne to conclude that man must not
kill any creatures at all or that all creatures are of equal
value. Yet he does recommend killing other creatures only
with reluctance, while at the same time acknowledging
that a man is vastly more significant to nature (and thus
to God) than an ant.[33]

By means of his doctrines of sociality and altruism
Hartshorne believes that he destroys any possible basis
for a self-defeating atomistic and solipsistic human individualism. To paraphrase the Apostle Paul, Hartshorne
believes that no man should or could live unto himself or
die unto himself. Nevertheless, while avoiding the Scylla
of individualism, he also strives mightily to steer clear
of the Charybdis of all forms of collectivism. As we have
been led to expect, he denies that even man's intimate
and ultimate relationship to God could ever rob man of
his essential freedom and independence. Moreover, he
also rejects any collective or "group mind," whether of
family, nation, or race, above the human individual and

below the mind of God in which human freedom and individuality could be submerged.[34] Hence, the way would appear to be open for free and responsible human social existence.

According to Hartshorne, each momentary human self is free by definition. If these selves are not partially capable of self-determination and thus partly free to wish, choose, and act in independence of the rest of the universe, then they are not distinct selves at all but are indistinguishable from a cosmic causal system.[35] Similarly, as explained above, Hartshorne holds that love in the form of sympathy, either immediate or mediate, is a fundamental feature of the human condition and of the total cosmos. Indeed, he insists upon the supremacy of love, suggesting that this insistence is a clear indication of the superiority of his panpsychism over metaphysical materialisms and dualisms. Without love, human life is not worth living. But have not those cosmologies that describe the universe as mostly blind, dead, loveless matter and those biologies that conceive all animal life as ruthless power struggles vehemently denied the possibility and relevance of love for human life? Still further, Hartshorne points out that our loveless physics and biology have produced in our time loveless politics and economics, with the results that we have seen the revival of human cruelty on an unprecedented scale and the adoption of callous economic policies which leave the alleviation of human miseries to the automatic functioning of the "market." [36] His view is that love and sympathy should be dominant conceptions in all human endeavors, whether they be metaphysical, physical, political, economic, or what-not.

Love, therefore, to Hartshorne, is a conceptually uni-

fying and morally purifying concept. As the supreme
ethical standard, and as the universal essence of actual
events, the single principle of love is the master key to
the understanding of *both* facts and values.[37] He denies
that any human institutions, churches included, could be
infallible; but he affirms that we can infallibly know "the
appropriateness of love." [38] In his praise of love, Hartshorne extols it as the sharing of the sufferings of others
that is our only consolation in the face of tragedy which
is the inevitable concomitant of all experience. Moreover,
he corrects Plato, who said that love is the search for
supreme beauty, and declares that love simply *is* the
supreme beauty.[39] In addition, he avers that the whole
range of emotional and aesthetic experiences in whatever
sensory form can be interpreted most illuminatingly as
the manifestations and self-enjoyment of love.[40]

The reader may be tempted by Hartshorne's glorifica-
tion of love and sympathy to think of him as a sheer senti-
mentalist. If so, he should read Hartshorne's "Note" at
the conclusion of *Reality as Social Process*, published in
1953.[41] There he speaks of pacifism as "error" and affirms his conviction that the United States should not
renounce the use either of strategic bombing or nuclear
weapons in its "Cold War" with Russia. He suggests that
the horrible nature of such military tactics may be more
than counterbalanced by the horror of other means of
warfare or of being an enslaved people. Moreover, he
argues that, since tragedy is an ingredient in every situation, there are no easy solutions to our military and diplo-
matic quandaries. However, he does recommend more
reliance upon imaginative diplomacy than upon weap-
onry; and he also decries the use of terror bombing of

civilian populations, as was sometimes employed by the United States in World War II, in even the fiercest of wars.

THE NATURE OF IMMORTALITY

That Hartshorne believes a thoroughgoing analysis of the nature of man always leads to consideration of the reality of God is most clearly seen in his discussion of the question of human immortality. He regards death as man's inevitable destiny which we must all face; but how can we face it? For the nonbeliever in God, the only feasible notion of immortality seems to be a "social immortality" or an "immortality of influence" upon one's posterity, somewhat similar to that held by the ancient Israelites and by Aristotle. However, Hartshorne effectively catalogues the inadequacies of this view of immortality through posterity. For instance, if the human race eventually ceases to exist (and modern science forecasts this eventuality), then one will lose all his posterity and his "immortality." Furthermore, even if the race survives forever, posterity remembers very little about the lives of only a very few of its predecessors. Still further, and most tellingly, not even one's contemporaries can understand adequately the full range, depth, and quality of one's life. Therefore, immortality in posterity appears to be a completely unsatisfactory answer to the question of human destiny—unless, as Hartshorne advocates, God as the divine survivor of all deaths is included among one's posterity.[42]

Concerning the survival of the human personality after death, whether in the Platonic sense of the immortality

of the soul or the biblical sense of the resurrection of
the body, Hartshorne is at times agnostic and at others
quite skeptical. Certainly, he considers the question of a
post-mortem prolongation of personal experiences as a
decidedly subsidiary and problematic issue.[43] The idea
that the human self could, after death, go on having experiences in an unlimited forever seems to him to smack
too much of making man into an angel or a God;
therefore, Hartshorne avows that this is impossible.[44] Especially repugnant to Hartshorne's sensibilities is the traditional belief that, after death, human beings spend an
eternity in either bliss or torment, consciously enjoying
rewards for good deeds done in this life or agonizingly
enduring punishment for misdeeds. He admits that the
traditional theory of heaven and hell might have conveyed
certain spiritual truths, but he also insists that the whole
idea is largely "a colossal error and one of the most
dangerous that ever occurred to the human mind . . . ."[45]
Hartshorne seems to hold that we shall engage in no personal actions at all after death; and, as for rewards and
punishments, he declares his rather unconventional conviction that they are all received in the now of the present
moment of action and at no other time or place.[46]

Furthermore, Hartshorne's main point in this connection is that, even if death were postponed indefinitely or
if people had an infinite series of experiences beyond
death, the central question of whether or not our lives
have any permanent value would still remain unanswered.
Consistently with his entire philosophy of social process,
he asserts that the main values of life are in the *experiences* of living, but these experiences vanish from our
grasp and memory every second. Does this mean that all

my previous experiences are now forgotten and lost forever? If so, then my life cannot have any enduring meaning or value. Therefore, to Hartshorne the question of immortality is paramountly a question of the immortality of personal *experiences* and not of persons.

What, then, is Hartshorne's answer to the question of immortality? Have the vanished experiences of dead men and of living men perished forevermore? "By no means!" he exclaims. They are all everlastingly preserved in their total value, exactly as originally experienced, in the everlasting and omniscient memory of God. Once an experience has occurred, it can never really perish, for it is indelibly imprinted upon the all-retaining tablet of God's memory throughout his literally everlasting future life. Man may forget, but God forgets nothing. Consequently, every feeling-event of our lives is a contribution to the memory and experience of God; and the chief questions for us to ask are whether our contributions to God's everlasting treasury are worthy or unworthy. God, as "the cosmically social being," imperishably knows and loves every actual experience of feeling in all its unique nuances with unfailing zest and fidelity. This "objective immortality" of all experiences in God is for Hartshorne the only adequate solution to the problem. Apart from God, therefore, life would be without enduring value.[47] With God, human life from conception to death is an "innumerable caravan" of experiences that irresistibly move beyond the grasp of human awareness toward their perpetual preservation as everlastingly real in the divine remembrance. "The true immortality is everlasting fame before God."[48]

In addition to settling positively and affirmatively the question of the enduring value of human life, Hartshorne's

conception of immortality can lay claim to other merits.
First, it unravels the mystery of death. Death becomes
not the sheer destruction or obliteration of life but merely
its termination, the setting of a limit to the total number
of indestructible experiences that comprise a given life.[49]
Secondly, in urging upon man the principle that his actions help determine the nature of God's everlasting memory of him, it gives very powerful inducement to highly
moral and unselfish living within a cosmic perspective.[50]
Finally, it affirms a cosmic basis for absolutely cherishing
the worth of life's every moment, inasmuch as "each moment of life is an end in itself, and not just a means to
some future goal." [51] In consequence, therefore, of all
these principles, one cannot detect in Hartshorne's doctrine of man even the faintest traces of despair of life's
ultimate meaning, fear or perplexity in the face of death,
moral vertigo, or denigration of the enduring value of our
transient earthly life.

In summation of this chapter, we can do no better than
employ once again Hartshorne's own words:

> To live everlastingly, as God does, can scarcely be our privi-
> lege; but we may earn everlasting places as lives well lived
> within the one life that not only evermore will have been
> lived, but evermore and inexhaustibly will be lived in ever
> new ways.[52]

IV. What Is Supreme Reality?

"They too have supposed that Deity must be the transcendental snob, or the transcendental tyrant, either ignoring the creatures or else reducing them to his mere puppets, rather than the unsurpassably interacting, loving, presiding genius and companion of all existence."
—*A Natural Theology for Our Time.*

Charles Hartshorne deserves the title "the God-intoxicated philosopher" as much as any thinker since Spinoza. Moreover, the extent and intensity of his lifetime of concentration upon the questions of the nature and existence of God have few equals in the history of philosophy. Beyond question, the animating spirit of the full range of his philosophizing has been essentially religious; and he has once suggested that philosophy is "the rational element in religion." [1] With the broad perspective of one gifted with metaphysical genius, he affirms that an adequate philosophy of religion can only be developed within the framework of a comprehensive general philosophy; but the elaboration of his system makes clear that the doctrine of God is not just one facet but, as with Aristotle, the very zenith of his cosmology. In fact, Hartshorne explicitly states that, on the most fundamental level, the question of God is the *sole* question of metaphysics. [2] And

73

few informed persons would wish to deny that his neoclassical metaphysics makes it possible to develop a radically new conceptualization of God—a conceptualization
sorely needed in our time.

Nevertheless, although Hartshorne does demonstrate
that metaphysics definitely can illuminate theology, his
most profound lesson has been that right thinking about
God can shed amazing light upon the entire metaphysical
landscape. Accordingly, he declares that the knowledge
of God is "the only adequate organizing principle of our
life and thought." [3] With force and effectiveness, nearly
all of his works drive home the point that both man and
nature point inevitably toward God and are incomprehensible apart from him. Previous chapters have already
explained why he believes that thorough exploration of the
questions of a cosmic mind in nature and of human immortality lead necessarily to the question of God; but we
must now endeavor to delineate the full sweep of his philosophical theology as the climax of his cosmology.

THE INADEQUACIES OF HUMANISM

In spite of what he considers to be its grievous limitations,
it is evident that Hartshorne is favorably impressed by
some aspects of atheistic humanism. He frequently acknowledges that there are assets as well as liabilities in
the philosophies of such influential atheistic humanists
as Karl Marx, Sigmund Freud, George Santayana, John
Dewey, Bertrand Russell, and others. As especially noteworthy contributions of humanism, he cites such achievements as the protest against intellectual dishonesty in
religion, encouragement of scientific research, insistence

that love of God by theists should include love of man, concentration of attention upon man's earthly life, and promotion of the values of humility and kindness.[4]

Nevertheless, Hartshorne is also a powerful critic of humanism. He repeatedly insists that no form of atheistic humanism could possibly be a satisfactory philosophy for the masses of mankind in the long run. His chief reason for this insistence is that humanism cannot withstand a searching philosophical analysis. According to him, all atheistic philosophies, when weighed in the scales of fundamental metaphysics, are found wanting. He locates humanism's main defects at the level of intellectual confusion and short-sightedness. As far as he is concerned, all atheistic humanisms fail to perceive that humanity cannot support itself alone in an indifferent or hostile universe. It seems obvious that human life cannot be fruitfully lived on the merely human level; and, therefore, humanism, when thoroughly consistent, defeats its own aims. Moreover, Hartshorne believes that his entire philosophy is a demonstration that the aims of humanism may be fully achieved only on the basis of neoclassical theism.

By the term "humanism" Hartshorne means the belief that man is the highest type of individual in existence and that "God" can only properly mean the noblest aspects of humanity. He also observes that it claims that man is essentially alone in the universe and that he is better off if he is made fully aware of this loneliness.[5] However, Hartshorne enters the counterclaim that, if man believes that he really is all by himself in an unfriendly universe, then man will realize that he is not worthy of his own supreme devotion and will also become an easy prey for the race-

worship and nation-worship that wreak havoc on mankind.[6]
He further charges that humanism suffers from the specific
disease of "megalomania" or wishing to be God.[7]

Indeed, Hartshorne's catalogue of ills that afflict those
who have lost faith in nature and God as friends is a fright-
ful list: "men are likely to grow bitter, or depressed and
fearful, or genially cynical and selfish, or mad with mega-
lomaniac ambition, or slavishly worshipful of power or
wealth—or just dull and apathetic and unimaginative, like
a number of agnostics I have known." [8] Moreover, he says
that those humanists who, like Bertrand Russell in "A Free
Man's Worship," respond with defiance of nature and
man's fate, are only engaging in exercises in futility. Man's
intelligence raises the question of the long-range destiny of
human life and values, and the honest humanist can only
answer that all alike are destined for oblivion. Therefore,
humanism denies the possibility of a permanent unity between man and nature; and it asserts that, in the long run,
no human actions or values will make any difference whatever.[9] And Hartshorne expostulates that such a creed is
impossible for man to live by.

In an impressive study entitled "Humanism as Disinte-
gration," [10] Hartshorne argues further that humanism
cannot but fail to achieve the integration of human
personality. No personality, says he, can satisfactorily adjust to the thought of a future time when all its values will
have vanished and all his achievements be just as if they
never had been. Thus man cannot live a unified life apart
from belief in the divine memory of all things past.

Moreover, Hartshorne contends that the finite personality
cannot soberly adjust to its own finitude but will suffer
from some form of megalomania, unless it knows itself to

be in the presence of an actually infinite reality that understands and loves it. Still further, in a specially interesting point, he asserts that humanism cannot synthesize for persons both knowledge and love. This inability derives from the fact that the humanist can really love only mankind but needs to know all of nature, thus requiring of man a loveless knowledge of nature. Indeed, Hartshorne reasons that humanism cannot even integrate the notion of knowledge itself. The only thing that a purposive rational mind can fully understand is another such mind, and, therefore, to assert that nature is godless is to deny that it can be intelligible to man. Finally, Hartshorne stresses the ethical and social defectiveness of humanism: if the total universe and even human bodies are essentially loveless machines driven by blind forces, "then it is impossible that the conception of spirit or love should have more than a very fitful hold upon us." [11]

Nevertheless, Hartshorne employs more than a strategy of negative critique of humanism. He also constructs a strong case for his thesis that belief in God is the only alternative to a hopeless paradoxicality of language. His position is that intensive analysis of all the fundamental categories of language discloses either unavoidable paradoxes or the reality of God as an indispensable aspect of the categories' meanings.[12] In his own words, "Language is bound to generate paradox if one attempts to purify it of all theistic implications; standard language is essentially theistic." [13] In fact, Hartshorne suggests the propriety of regarding theism itself as just the full elucidation of the categorical meanings of unavoidable linguistic terms.[14]

For Hartshorne, all such terms as "causality," "matter,"

"mind," "private," "knowable," "ordered," "good,"
"evil," "the past," and "certainty," cannot be understood
as having any clear, unparadoxical meaning apart from
God as depicted by neoclassical metaphysics. For example, in the specific case of privacy, what sense does it make
to talk of your feelings as being either like or unlike mine,
since an objective comparison between them can never
take place? Hartshorne's reply is that it makes no sense at
all—unless all private states are directly known by God
who actually does make the comparison in question.[15]

Therefore, for all the foregoing reasons and for others
that have not been stated, Hartshorne holds that humanism
is incapable of ever doing full justice to the depths and
implications of the human existence which it prizes so
highly.

THE INCONSISTENCIES OF CLASSICAL THEISM

As we have already indicated, although Hartshorne ad-
judges humanism to be inadequate, he does hail its laud-
able traits. However, the tradition of Western classical
theism does not fare quite so well under his critical scru-
tiny. It is only slight exaggeration to state that he feels the
traditional Western religious and philosophical understanding of God to be such a mass of errors and inconsistencies as to require removal *in toto* from the body of
metaphysical thought. In fact, he regards the traditional
doctrine of God as so rationally untenable that, if it were
the only conceivable notion of God, he would himself be
driven to adopt atheistic humanism in spite of its short-
comings.

In a word, what Hartshorne finds so repugnant to both

sound logic and true religion in the classical Western doctrine of God is the idea that God is an Absolute Being of Changeless Perfection. He maintains that this notion was the bastard child which resulted from the wedding of Greek metaphysics with the highest religious truth of the Bible. Among the chief officiators at this unfortunate (according to Hartshorne) union were such giant philosophical or theological minds as Philo, Augustine, Anselm, Aquinas, Descartes, and Kant.[16] In Hartshorne's judgment, the doctrine that God is "a being in *all* respects absolutely perfect or unsurpassable" [17] is the source of the trouble. Moreover, with logical rigor and religious zeal, he proceeds to demonstrate that this doctrine involves traditional theism in a whole raft of paradoxes and inner contradictions, in the hope that he might encourage its entire abandonment by thoughtful people.

What are some of the inherent inconsistencies of traditional theism? Following Hartshorne's extended discussion in his *Man's Vision of God and the Logic of Theism*,[18] we shall cite six examples related to God's absoluteness, omnipotence, changelessness, omniscience, love, and bliss. First, if God's absoluteness is total and "perfect," then he cannot be related to or relative to the world and man. But this means that God is completely unmoved and untouched by any good or evil which man may do and that man can make absolutely no difference to God. Yet, when judged by biblical and religious insight, such consequences seem patently false or absurd. They are especially repellent to Hartshorne, who feels that one of the highest religious motivations is the desire which man may have of doing some action in order to bring joy to the heart of God. Moreover, he also suggests that, when a man such as

Beethoven creates new forms of beauty in the universe, his creativity makes a difference even to God by adding new values to his experience.[19]

In regard to omnipotence, simple analysis reveals at once that God cannot literally have "all" power if there are any other beings in the universe whatever. If there are any beings other than God, then they must have at least some minute amount of power. Otherwise, they would not be beings at all; for what is a being with absolutely no power at all? Hartshorne readily allows that God may be *supremely* powerful; but, in a world of creatures, it does seem plain that he cannot be literally *"all*-powerful." [20]

In the third place, that God is completely changeless in every respect seems to follow from the idea of his perfection. If he is already totally perfect, how could he change at all, since any change would either imply or produce imperfection? But since the state of the world changes every moment, must not the states of a loving, wise, and concerned God also change each moment in response to the changes in the world process? Possibly some aspects of God's character and his constant adequacy may be unchanging, but surely not all aspects of God's being and action.[21]

Next, if God's "omniscience" is taken to mean that he knows all things that actually *are*, then Hartshorne agrees that God is omniscient. However, he argues that such an attribute cannot be extended to include God's specific foreknowledge of all or even any future events, inasmuch as no future events are now actual or real in such a manner that God could know them. For instance, how could God now know who "is" (from the standpoint of eternity) the fiftieth president of the United States, since there is not yet any determinate entity in either the present or the future? [22]

Fifthly, as far as Christians are concerned, Hartshorne's logic is probably most telling in regard to God's love. If God truly loves man, then it seems plain that he has some desires or "passions" and that he cannot be absolutely independent and immutable. What sense would it make to speak of God's love at all if it did not mean that he *wants* man's well-being and *responds* to both man's obedience and his waywardness? [23]

In the sixth place, it must be obvious that, if God's love is real, then his bliss cannot be absolute and perfect. Surely, God is displeased by man's sinfulness, weeps over human folly and cruelty, and suffers with mankind in its manifold agonies. How then can we seriously affirm that he dwells in perfect bliss? [24] And how indeed could Western Christianity and theism have defended for so many centuries a conception of God so glaringly inconsistent with itself and inimical to the biblical portrayal of God as the heavenly Father who grieves over his estranged children?

In *The Divine Relativity*, Hartshorne develops a similar critique of traditional theism, being especially concerned to deny that all God's attributes must be necessary as well as absolute. He convincingly demonstrates that some of God's properties must be contingent if there are any contingent events or truths in the world. He reasons thus: if God's knowledge that I exist is necessary knowledge, then my existence must be a necessity in God; but surely my existence is contingent existence, and, therefore, God's knowledge of my existence must be contingent also. The supposition that God might have necessary knowledge of contingent truths Hartshorne would classify as a sad case of religiously motivated semantical nonsense.[25]

Nevertheless, it would be a mistake to assume that Hartshorne believes that careful human reasoning could ever attain exhaustive knowledge of God's nature without any remainder of mystery. On the contrary, he admits that there is no lack of theological mystery and that the reality of God is so vast that our fullest knowledge of him must be infinitesimally small by comparison. His vigorous objection is directed to the kind of theological thought that glories in alleged "insuperable paradoxes" about God without recognizing that some "paradoxes" are actually impossible contradictions and others are excuses for slovenly thinking. In one of his more sarcastic moods, Hartshorne defines a "theological paradox" as "what a contradiction becomes when it is about God rather than something else . . ."! [26]

DIPOLAR THEISM

Hartshorne's own constructive doctrine of God claims to correct the inadequacies of atheistic humanism and to avoid the contradictions of classical theism. As a matter of fact, his contention is that the emergence of neoclassical theism marks the beginning of an entirely new era in man's thought about God. Moreover, he avers that, in the new theological era which has been inaugurated by process philosophy, neoclassical theism has thrust a new conception of God into the arena of debate, with the result that most previous descriptions of God are outmoded and must now be reworked. The bulk of Hartshorne's numerous writings is a strenuous argument that the only viable theological options open for man today are either neoclassical theism or thoroughgoing skepticism. And most of those

who have taken the trouble to investigate fairly Hartshorne's claims have been led to conclude that his version of
theology is indeed a novel, rich, and profoundly subtle
doctrine.

One will always misunderstand Hartshorne's doctrine of
God as long as he tries to conceive of God's being as
simple. His view is that the nature of God is irreducibly
complex. To be exact, he says that there are two aspects or
poles (hence the term "dipolar") to God's nature and that
neither pole can be comprehended apart from the other.
Tersely expressed, God has both an abstract facet and a
concrete facet. The abstract aspect of God is his absolute,
eternal, and necessary *existence;* and, as such, this aspect
can be known by abstract metaphysical argument and logical proof. On the other hand, the concrete aspect of God
is his dependent, related, and contingent *actuality;* and it,
being entirely inaccessible to rational proof, can only be
known by direct, empirical observation or "encounter." [27]
Moreover, the concrete aspect of deity is greater than the
abstract aspect and includes the latter within itself. Indeed, the abstract aspect of God is an unavoidable abstraction from his concrete actual experiences. Thus, despite
the awkward phrase, "the abstract-concrete God" (or "the
concrete-abstract God") is the simplest designation for God
that avoids distortion of Hartshorne's intentions.

The duality or polarity in God's nature, when fully
expounded, will be seen as the neoclassical theme that
runs through every movement of the Hartshornian metaphysical symphony. For Hartshorne, the reality of God
necessarily includes both his abstract existence and his
concrete actuality. However, the reality of God so all-
pervasively involves the total universe that to comprehend

divine reality means simply to comprehend all the reality
there is. The bare existence of God is the ultimate metaphysical abstraction, being correlative with the possibility
of anything whatever. It is thus totally nonspecific and
capable of being correlated with any situation whatsoever;
and this quality gives to it both absolute independence
and infinite flexibility or relativity.[28]

Consequently, Hartshorne emphasizes that the *existence*
of God is not a "state of affairs" that makes any recog-
nizable difference in the world. As the ultimate Principle
of possibility, a necessary feature of both actuality and
nonactuality, it is the *source* of all states of affairs in the
universe. In other language, God's existence is not a fact
but rather the principle of possibility of all facts. However, the *actuality* of God is related to the actuality of all
things at a given moment and is also the Supreme Fact or
State of affairs.[29]

Hartshorne seems to have arrived at his notion of a
dipolar deity by adaptation of Morris Cohen's "Law of
Polarity" for purposes of defending Whitehead's famous
distinction between the primordial and the consequent na-
tures of God. The Law of Polarity dictates that not just one
but *both* components of pairs of ultimate contraries should
be affirmed as true because they are mutually interdependent and correlative.[30] Accordingly, Hartshorne, in obeying
this law, insists that God is both absolute and relative,
infinite and finite, individual and universal, active and
passive, eternal and temporal, cause and effect, creative
and created, et cetera. Moreover, he suggests that most traditional theisms and pantheisms have been vitiated by fail-
ure to observe this law. They seem to have suffered from
the "monopolar prejudice," i.e., from the determination

to assert of deity that one of a pair of contraries is true and the other is false.[31]

Examples of the monopolar prejudice would be those theisms that have insisted that God is active but not passive, necessary but not contingent, independent but not dependent, and cause but not effect. Naturally, they believed that they were denying notions that were unworthy of deity when they said that God is not passive, contingent, dependent, and effect; but Hartshorne labels such belief as pure prejudice. Why should it be considered more divine for God merely to act upon the world and not also to be acted upon by the world, or to be changeless and not also changing, or to have the world depend upon him and not also depend upon the world? Hartshorne replies that the preferred contraries only appear more worthy of God to those suffering from an overdose of the Greek metaphysics of permanence and immutability, whereas neoclassical metaphysics enables one to realize that the rejected contraries may be even more deserving of attribution to God than their favored partners.

Therefore, he seeks to replace monopolarity with dipolarity in all thought concerning God. Moreover, his intention is that his theology should be truly dipolar and not deemphasize either pole of a pair of ultimate contraries. Thus, contrary to a common misunderstanding, Hartshorne does not stress the divine becoming to the exclusion of the divine being. Rather, he asserts that both being and becoming apply to God, the divine becoming only being more ultimate in the sense of more inclusive and concrete than the divine being.[32]

But does not dipolar thinking regarding God involve Hartshorne in hopeless contradiction? He insists that the answer is negative. The contraries which he affirms of God are not contradictories, because each pole of a pair of contraries is asserted of a different aspect of God. Therefore, God is eternal in one aspect of his reality and temporal in another, and the same holds for infinite-finite, immutable-mutable, et cetera. For instance, God's actual knowledge is finite because it is limited to the actual world at a given time, but his potential knowledge is literally infinite because it knows the potentially infinite worlds as potential. In the same manner, we may conceive God as necessary because of all things in the abstract pole of his reality, for he is the principle of possibility of all things; but he is also the contingent effect of all things in his concrete pole, because his actuality changes with every changing actual state of the world.

Furthermore, Hartshorne's dipolar version of deity escapes many absurdities and the charge of being a doctrine of two gods through the principle of "categorical supremacy" or "dual transcendence." The point of this principle is that God is a radically unique individual in the most eminent sense. Therefore, he is different in principle from all other beings by virtue of being superior to them. His unique excellence means that he far surpasses every other reality in every aspect of both poles of his nature. Hence, every category that applies either to God's existence or his actuality applies as the supreme instance or the "supercase" of that category. God's existence, being, relativity, dependence, and love are all uniquely and supremely cases of categoric excellence. Otherwise, without this superiority in principle over all others, the deity of God would be compromised in fatal fashion. No matter what faults are his, Hartshorne's faith in the unique supremacy of God is absolutely beyond question.[33]

Apparently, Hartshorne's favorite method of formulating the idea of God's unique supremacy is in terms of "surpassingness." His formula is that God is "unsurpassable by another"; and from it he logically derives many of God's attributes such as his creative inexhaustibility and his being eternally without beginning or end.[34]

Nevertheless, Hartshorne is most explicit in affirming that God is not absolutely perfect in all respects, on the grounds that an absolutely perfect being is inconceivable and impossible. Absolute perfection would have to mean the complete actualization of all possible values and seems to be no more imaginable than a greatest possible number. Hartshorne reasons that it is literally impossible for God to actualize all possibilities, for they are infinite in number, and some of them are mutually incompatible. Even God cannot behold the illustrious career of Charles Hartshorne in *both* the twentieth and the thirtieth centuries.

Consequently, we seem driven to the conclusion that no final state of maximum perfection is possible. God's perfection must be a dynamic and continually growing one. In any given instant, God's attributes must be categoric instances that incomparably surpass those of all other beings; but God will perpetually surpass himself in every future instant as his successive states actualize more and more possibilities. Accordingly, Hartshorne speaks willingly of the relative perfection of God, a perfection that can never be fully maximized.[35] There will be no end to the creative process or to the dynamic ongoing life of God. Hartshorne states the reason:

The infinity of possibilities in God's nature is inexhaustible in actuality even by divine power, or any conceivable power. For each creative synthesis furnishes materials for a novel and richer synthesis.[36]

Therefore, God will always be "the All-surpassing One" who forever surpasses all other beings and himself in the everlasting creative advance.

Hartshorne also likes to define God in religious terminology as "the One Who Is Worshipped." Naturally, if God is deserving of human worship, he will be the All-surpassing One. But Hartshorne adds that the One who is properly worshiped will also be an all-inclusive being of universal love. Defining worship as "a consciously unitary response to life," he reasons that God must be the all-inclusive wholeness of the world, who is worshiped by an integrated human personality. If God were not all-inclusive of the world, then worshiping him would be a disintegrative instead of an integrative experience.[37]

Additionally, Hartshorne finds further evidence that God is all-inclusive love in the Jewish-Christian commandment to love the Lord God with all one's heart, soul, mind, and strength. On the basis of this commandment, he contends that God must include all other beings within himself. Otherwise, one could not literally love God with all his heart and also delight, for example, in the singing of birds. However, if birdsong is somehow encompassed within God's being, then taking delight in it would merely be a partial aspect of loving God with all one's strength. In fact, any response one makes to the universe would be a form of the worship and love of God. Moreover, Hartshorne suggests that this same commandment is strong evidence that the God whom we worship with our whole being is himself love. His reason is twofold: it seems impossible that man could love God with the totality of his being if God were himself unloving; and it also seems that God could not really know the world without loving or participating sympathetically in it.[38]

Hartshorne confesses his belief that the insight into God as universal love was most clearly perceived by the ancient Jews and by Jesus, but the distinctive aspect of his position is the claim that secular philosophy can demonstrate and partially explicate the truth that "God is love."[39] Of course, dipolar theism is his effort to unpack the metaphysical implications of "God is love." His conclusion is that metaphysics must maintain that the universe is held together by love or watch itself evaporate into thin air. Hence, the aphorism: "Cosmic being is cosmic experience, is cosmic sociality or love."[40]

"The metaphysics of love" is an appropriate label that Hartshorne is willing to accept for his philosophy. Furthermore, he asserts that the idea of God as love is "the supremely beautiful abstract idea."[41] But the assertion "God is love" is intended as a dipolar truth about God. That God necessarily loves all things Hartshorne understands as a necessary truth which metaphysics may demonstrate, whereas that God loves me or any specific creature is a contingent truth which only actual creaturely experience may discover or enjoy. Moreover, Hartshorne distinguishes between God's love for all creatures and his valuation of them. True, God must love all creatures equally, entering sympathetically and perfectly into the life of the lowliest insect as well as into the life of the greatest man; but this does not necessarily mean that God regards them both as of equal value. God may correctly

perceive that different creatures have different values but
still perfectly sympathize with the joys and sorrows of
each.[42]

Furthermore, not surprisingly, Hartshorne maintains
that the idea of God as all-inclusive of reality does not
entail the pantheistic implication that the creatures have
no real freedom in God. On the contrary, he argues that
the perfect love of God must be willing to respect the freedom and accept the decisions of the creatures as real without necessarily approving them. For love, it seems, involves
a willingness not only to act upon or for the beloved but
also to be molded by the beloved.[43]

Obviously, Hartshorne's deity is an eminently social
God who corresponds exactly with the social nature of all
reality. Indeed, it is not incorrect to say that God is the
love, or sympathy, or sociality of things. Since mind or
awareness is the most relational of all entities, Hartshorne
concludes that God as eminent mind is the supremely related, most dependent being of all.[44] Furthermore, because
he is the surpasser of all others, his sociality must be an
absolute relativity. Therefore, God by definition must be
incapable of not sharing sympathetically *all* other feelings. His experience is the most eminent form of "feeling
of feelings." "The eminent form of sympathetic dependence can only apply to deity, for this form cannot be less
than an omniscient sympathy, which depends upon and is
exactly colored by every nuance of joy or sorrow anywhere in the world." [45]

Moreover, God's eminent sociality entails his eminent
creativity. The ordinary sociality of actual occasions involves them creatively in influencing others; and, therefore,
God's supreme sociality must involve his supremely par-

ticipating in the creation of other events. And by the same logic of eminence, God must be the supreme case of being creatively dependent upon and shaped by the creativity of others.[46]

PANENTHEISM

"Panentheism" (literally meaning "all-in-God") and "Surrelativism" (short form of "Supreme-Relativism") are terms equivalent to "dipolar theism." Hartshorne uses all three terms interchangeably and with about the same relative frequency. However, "panentheism". explicitly contrasts with both "theism" and "pantheism," and it brings the relationship between God and the world into central focus. We use the term for the heading of this section in which the effort is made to render still more explicit Hartshorne's view of this mutual relationship between God and the world.

Hartshorne's position is that literally everything exists in God and that God, like the universe, has no external environment. All actualities are actual in God, and all potentialities are potential in God. "He is the Whole in every categorial sense, all actuality in one individual actuality, and all possibility in one individual potentiality." [47] Panentheism thus differs from traditional theism by asserting that all the world is entirely inside God instead of outside him; and it diverges from pantheism by insisting that the creatures which are all in God nevertheless have a measure of genuine freedom, independence, and even capacity for evil. In distinction from pantheism, panentheism also asserts that, besides the totality of ordinary causes and effects, God as the inclusive whole may

act as a distinct causal agent upon the parts which constitute him and the cosmos.[48] Moreover, panentheism includes
the notion that God's abstract essence or eternal existence
is logically independent of, and hence distinguishable
from, every particular world.[49]

The most important basis for the panentheistic insistence
that everything must exist *in* God rests upon a logical
analysis of the idea of divine omniscience coupled with a
belief regarding the nature of relations in general. The
argument runs as follows: God has knowledge of everything that exists, but to include relations within oneself
must mean to include the terms of the relations; therefore,
all that exists must exist within God, since God's relation
of knowledge of everything exists within himself.[50] The
crucially debatable premise is the statement that to include
relations must mean to include their terms, but this is a
highly technical point into which we cannot enter here.

However, we are now in position to understand why
Hartshorne and Reese, in their impressive study of conceptions of God entitled *Philosophers Speak of God*, define
the panentheistic deity as "The Supreme as Eternal-
Temporal Consciousness, Knowing and including the
World." [51] Hartshorne admits that human persons may
have knowledge of objects without embracing the objects
within their personal being, but he counters that human
knowledge is also fallible and imperfect. And in the case
of God, he feels it is obvious that God's actuality cannot
be something different from his knowledge and/or love
and their/its objects. Accordingly, he concludes that the
world apart from God is an abstraction from the cosmic
manifoldness as the integrated contents of the divine
omniscience.[52]

By what analogy shall we conceive the relationship between God and the world? Hartshorne suggests that there is only one truly illuminating possibility. Just as he holds that man must conceive the nature of "matter" as analogous to human unit-experiences, so he also says that the human mind-body relationship is about the only available analogy for the relationship between God and the world. Stated precisely, the analogy is that God is to the world as the human mind is to the human body. Or, the world is God's body, and God is the world's mind·or soul. As in the case of man, God (or the world) is a single, besouled organism. Hence, Hartshorne says that God has direct access to all parts of the world through immediate social relations after the fashion of human minds' being immediately aware of the states of their brain cells. Moreover, he declares that God is so highly exalted above the creatures that his immediate knowledge of all their states does not constitute a tyrannical or objectionable invasion of their rightful privacies.[53]

Naturally, employing the mind-body analogy for God's relationship to the world is ample warrant for speaking of God as the Supreme Person. Hartshorne often affirms his conviction that Whitehead erred in referring to God as an actual entity, because he believes that God is a *society* of actual entities or a "society of societies"; [54] but this latest suggestion might tend to impair the usefulness of the mind-body analogy. At any rate, Hartshorne states that, as with a human personality, the concrete divine personality is partially new each moment, with each new divine self remembering its predecessors and anticipating vaguely its successors.[55] However, he has little to say concerning how long a "moment" might be for God. Still it is because of

the notion of God as Eminent Person that Hartshorne may
bluntly pronounce, "Theology is an attempted psychology
of deity." [56]

What does the panentheistic deity do for the world?
Two things: he infallibly preserves each successive cosmic
and subcosmic event in his perpetual memory, thereby
rendering it immortal; and he gives order and guidance
through inspiration to the creatures in the next phase of
the creative process.[57] Hartshorne adopts the Whiteheadian
view that God may really rule the world but that he does
so chiefly by persuasion. God may order the world and
set the limits beyond which freedom may not go. His social
awareness results in action that prevents any unsocial be-
havior (e.g., Hitler) from getting entirely out of hand.
That is, God may exercise a predominant-if-not-total influence upon the creatures and thus set relatively narrow
limits to their freedom. Moreover, his influence is a form
of persuasion, because he sets new ideals and orders of
preference for each successive moment of creaturely
existence.

However, the divine persuasion can only be effective if
the creatures are aware of God's feelings and desires each
moment. Such awareness is exactly what Hartshorne affirms as the case. He holds that all subsequent actual
entities feel God's actual experiences in some deficient
manner and, therefore, that we take our cues for this
moment largely by knowing what God presently desires.[58]
Hartshorne's own words are pertinent:

> God orders the universe, according to panentheism, by taking
> into his own life all the currents of feeling in existence. He
> is the most irresistible of influences precisely because he is
> himself the most open to influence. In the depths of their

hearts all creatures (even those able to "rebel" against him) defer to God because they sense him as the one who alone is adequately moved by what moves them. He alone not only knows but feels (the only adequate knowledge, where feeling is concerned) how they feel, and he finds his own joy in sharing their lives, lived according to their own free decisions, not fully anticipated by any detailed plan of his own. Yet the extent to which they can be permitted to work out their own plan depends on the extent to which they can echo or imitate on their own level the divine sensitiveness to the needs and precious freedom of all. In this vision of a deity who is not a supreme autocrat, but a universal agent of "persuasion," whose "power is the worship he inspires" (Whitehead), that is, flows from the intrinsic appeal of his infinitely sensitive and tolerant relativity, by which all things are kept moving in orderly togetherness, we may find help in facing our task of today, the task of contributing to the democratic self-ordering of a world whose members not even the supreme orderer reduces to mere subjects with the sole function of obedience.[59]

In panentheism, God's supreme relativity definitely means that God is a cocreator of man and the world and also that man is a cocreator of himself *and of God*. Each concrete state of God partially just springs into actuality spontaneously, but it is also partially produced by the prior states of God and of the world (including man).[60] However, the influence of any single creature upon God is so slight that the momentary influence of the totality of creatures can never deprive God of his eminent freedom. Nevertheless, although Hartshorne asserts that all creatures participate in the universal creativity of self and others, with God as creator in the eminent sense, he specifically repudiates the classical Christian idea that God created the world *ex nihilo* or "out of nothing." Panentheism en-

tails that there never could have been God without a
world. Therefore, it rejects the idea of a first state of
creation or a beginning of the universe. In addition, it
affirms that every state of the universe has been created
out of a previous state in the everlasting creative advance
of God and the world which literally had no beginning
and shall have no end.[61]

Perhaps the most notable and striking contrast between
traditional theism and Hartshorne's panentheism is the latter's unflinching avowal of the suffering of God as a poignantly real and everlastingly unavoidable facet of divine
experience. The suffering of God follows inevitably from
the notions of his omniscient awareness and the world's
genuinely free capacity to produce suffering, tragedy, and
evil. Therefore, the Christian doctrine of the Cross is raised
to a metaphysical dimension, and God is seen to be totally
vulnerable instead of wholly immune to suffering.[62]

Hartshorne's position is that every actual entity or society of entities has some freedom that not even God can
entirely control. Thus there is a division of powers and of
responsibility in the universe that has tragic implications
for both the universe and God.[63] God may set the limits for
the creaturely decisions, but he does not make their decisions for them; and inherent in the free decisions of the
creatures are possibilities for both good and evil. A mul-
tiplicity of actual entities, each with a measure of free
self-determination, presents an irremovable risk of conflict
as well as opportunity for harmony. Accordingly, every
new phase of the everlasting world process will afford
more possibilities for evil, and evil will never be totally
eliminated from the universe and the experience of God.[64]

The fact of evil is, therefore, a sobering reality which

God can mitigate but not eradicate, but neither is its presence God's will or responsibility. The free decisions of creatures for evil and good become the destiny of other creatures and of God. Hence, "there is chance and tragedy even for God." [65] Moreover, God's omniscient awareness deprives him of the human luxury of remaining oblivious to the misery of others. He must share perfectly in miseries as well as joys of all creatures, preserving this painful awareness in everlasting memory. Thus he is radically dependent upon others for his happiness, for he must suffer when others either endure or produce suffering.[66] The panentheistic God perpetually actualizes himself both in the sublimely blissful joy of sharing the joys of others and in the cosmic crucifixion of feeling supreme sympathy for the agonies of all creatures. He is the cosmic Sufferer.

REASONS FOR BELIEF IN THE DIPOLAR GOD

As was stated in the preceding section, Hartshorne maintains that every actual entity is aware of the nature of God, at least in some deficient manner. He reasons that, as the universal and necessary principle of all existence, God must be present as a datum in every experience whatever, regardless of whether or not the experiencing subject is fully conscious of this presence. Therefore, he affirms that there is a latent awareness of God in the depths of every man. He also asserts that it is impossible for any man or animal to be totally unaware of deity. Hence, the difference between believer and unbeliever is one of different levels of awareness and self-understanding, with Hartshorne holding that it is the unbeliever who misunderstands or confuses the fundamental nature of his experiences.[67]

Furthermore, although Hartshorne believes that everyone
actually has some faith in God, he points out that some of
the traditional philosophical proofs for the existence of
God, when revised to fit the neoclassical deity, may be
relevant and useful in bringing to the level of conscious
thought the awareness of God which all men feel. Moreover, he opines that these proofs are essentially arguments
that reduce to absurdity any alternatives to panentheism
by demonstrating their incoherence or vacuousness.[68]
Moreover, the proofs may show that the idea of the dipolar
deity or the Unsurpassable Object of our worship is not
nonsense.[69]

Hartshorne declares that there are many possible valid
arguments for the existence of God, but his writings con-
centrate on perfecting various forms of neoclassical versions of the traditional "ontological" and "cosmological"
proofs. Moreover, he has probably given more prolonged
and intensive thought to the ontological argument than
any other philosopher in history, and his studies have con-
tributed notably to a recent revival of interest in it. As a
result, both philosophers and theologians are now giving
more serious attention to this and other theistic arguments
than they have given in many decades.

Of course, a thorough exploration of the profundities of
Hartshorne's development of the ontological argument
alone is much beyond the scope of the present study. He
himself has written hundreds of pages on the subject.[70]
However, it will be within our purpose to explain generally
how his treatment of the theistic arguments accords exactly
with his neoclassical understanding of God.

The most essential step toward understanding Hartshorne's development of both the ontological and the cos-

mological arguments is to keep well in mind that the deity whose existence he is trying to prove is dipolar in nature. And the existence of the dipolar deity is just one pole of his being, namely, the abstractly eternal and necessary pole. Hartshorne repeatedly reiterates his affirmation that the theistic arguments only demonstrate the *existence* of God and that they tell us nothing whatever about God's concrete actuality. The concrete actuality of God at any moment he considers to be entirely beyond the reach of metaphysical reason. Since the divine actuality is contingent, no proof can pertain to it. It can only be known through empirical observation and experience.[71]

If, accordingly, one clearly remembers that only God's abstract existence is in question, he can easily comprehend how a Hartshornian reformulation of the ontological argument is possible. In the eleventh century, Anselm of Canterbury gave the ontological argument its classical expression. In the second and possibly better of two formulations of this argument, he reasoned as follows: Since a being greater than God is by definition inconceivable, and since a being whose nonexistence is inconceivable is greater than a being whose nonexistence is conceivable, therefore, God must be a being whose nonexistence is inconceivable.

A typical Hartshornian restatement of Anselm's argument in the language of modern modal logic runs about like this: Since God is by definition not conceivably surpassable, and since a being whose existence is necessary surpasses one whose existence is merely contingent, therefore, God's existence must be necessary existence. In other words, God as the Unsurpassable One cannot fail to exist, or the nonexistence of the Unsurpassable One is a self-contradictory concept. Hartshorne hails as Anselm's great discovery the ideas that God's mode of being is utterly unique in his perfection or unsurpassability and that contingent existence is inferior to necessary existence.[72]

The necessary existence of God may be readily understood as a self-evident truth in Hartshornian metaphysics. Hartshorne holds that the necessary is precisely the common denominator of all possible states of reality, but this common denominator *is* God's abstract existence as such. Hence, Hartshorne's formula that God is "necessarily somehow actualized."[73] The *how* of divine actualization is a contingently different fact each moment, but *that* God is actualized is an eternally necessary abstract truth. God's existence is the extreme abstraction from all the alternative concrete states of reality. That is, God's creativity is the ground of possibility or, as the common factor of all possibilities, is coextensive with possibility as such. Thus his existence must be necessary, for *every* possibility is a realization of divine potentiality. Therefore, no matter what happens, God must exist. Is it possible that there might be no possibility at all? The very thought seems absurd or impossible. Therefore, God must exist necessarily. That is to say, possibility is a necessity![74]

It deserves emphasis that Hartshorne's understanding of God's necessary existence means that this divine existence does not make any empirical difference whatever in the world. It is the ground of all differences and of any possible world. God's existence does not compete with the existence of any other individuals whatever, for it is compatible with any sort of actuality at all. It does not necessitate that any specific entity either exist or not exist but only that *something* exist. God's momentary actualities are determinate and do exclude many things, but his existence is absolutely flexible.[75]

Consequently, since God's existence is not a question of fact, then it must be a question of meaning, i.e., a properly metaphysical question. Therefore, Hartshorne believes that the ontological argument has the great merit of not only recalling philosophers to their central metaphysical task but also of greatly clarifying the issues of theistic belief. The clarification of theistic belief comes from the fact that the argument has eliminated the possibility of empirical atheism and empirical theism. If God's existence is not a factual question at all, then obviously nothing about the world and the experience of it could possibly either disprove his existence or prove it. Therefore, there seem to be only two possibilities left on the field, theism or positivism. By explicating the meaning of God as the Unsurpassable One, the ontological argument excludes the possibility of God's nonexistence. The only alternatives that remain are either to affirm that "God" means necessary existence or means nothing at all (or is nonsense).[76] Hence Hartshorne's conclusion that the only logical way left to reject theism is not to deny the existence of God but to affirm that the very idea of God is either vacuous or self-contradictory.[77]

Hartshorne asserts that, because the question of God's existence is a question of meaning, there are as many possible arguments for God's existence as there are purely general categories. Any such conception as knowledge, value, actuality, truth, goodness, or beauty could, by proper analysis, be shown to imply the others and the necessity of God's existence. Therefore, he holds that any valid theistic argument is sufficient, since they are all interdependent on the nonempirical, metaphysical level.[78]

Hartshorne's cosmological argument runs in this fashion: the undeniable reality of change and process implies that God eternally exists as the subject of all change, for otherwise there could be no genuine change at all. In other words, *what* changes if God does not exist necessarily? An alternative formulation is that the world as a unity is explainable only by the divinely inclusive love that binds the many into a single cosmic structure; and, therefore, the world of secular experience is nonsense if God does not exist.[79] Similarly, one neoclassical version of the traditional teleological argument would be that the fact that the world has any order at all is only to be explained by an eternal divine Orderer, because apart from God it is impossible to understand why chaos and anarchy are not unlimited and supreme.[80]

In summation: "Apart from God not only would this world not be conceivable, but no world, and no state of reality, or even of unreality, could be understood." [81] That is, one cannot think deeply and adequately about the world without thinking of God. Likewise, one cannot think of God without conceiving of the world. God and the world imply each other at the fundamental metaphysical level, each being the same thing from a different perspective. Therefore, we may appropriately conclude this survey of Hartshorne's creatively novel conception of God with a quotation that epitomizes his central metaphysical insights: "The only possible argument for God must show that doubt of God is doubt of any and all truth, renunciation of the essential categories of thinking." [82]

V. A Critical Evaluation
of Hartshorne's Philosophy

"I have a certain faith in the rights and duties of
rational metaphysical inquiry."
—*A Natural Theology for Our Time.*

In this final chapter, a brief critical assessment of Hartshorne's philosophy will be our aim. This writer's overall
reaction to the total impact of Hartshorne's work is over-
whelmingly favorable and positive, but not uncritical.
Hartshorne has a message that we all need to hear. For
too long, he has been considered as something of a philosophical maverick or theological "sport" and has therefore been politely ignored. Fortunately, however, this
situation is rapidly changing, and both philosophers and
theologians are increasingly willing to give earnest attention to his thought. Some will be converted by the power
of his reason to some kind of process philosophy and/or
theology, while others will glean from him significant new
insights to be incorporated into their own more traditional
perspectives. But all who pay the price of diligent concentration upon his philosophy will be rewarded for their
labors. No matter whether one finally jumps on the Hartshornian bandwagon or not, the most important duty is to
hear him carefully and fairly. This is the chief reason why
the bulk of this volume has been primarily exposition of

his philosophical position, with critical comments being
kept to a minimum. Now, however, some evaluation is in
order.

Without intending to draw, in a definitely un-Harts-
hornian manner, a sharp distinction between philosophy
and theology, we may first develop our estimate of the
more philosophical issues in Hartshorne and then proceed
to the theological ones.

PHILOSOPHICAL ISSUES

As suggested in chapter one, Hartshorne pursues metaphysics in the grand style. Because of his confidence in
the powers of rigorous reasoning, he proceeds to paint a
metaphysical landscape that is in principle as wide as
reality. The result is an impressive metaphysical vision
à la Whitehead. Moreover, in our age of anxiety, irra-
tionality, and the absurd, it is exhilarating to behold a
comprehensive metaphysics in which everything fits together in coherent fashion. Hartshorne's trust in the wholeness of reason and the wholeness of man in the universe
is a refreshing reminder that man may at least still hope
that alienation and fragmentation are not the final descriptions of his existence. In addition, Hartshorne's steady
contention in the philosophical arena that metaphysics
inevitably involves the question of God will not be regarded
as insignificant by those who believe, as I do, that man and
the world are incomprehensible apart from God.

Professor Langdon Gilkey has pointed out that a rational metaphysics such as Hartshorne's makes two important assumptions concerning reason. First, it assumes
that there is an objective rational or logos structure to the

entire universe; and, secondly, it presupposes that human reason may accurately and adequately know this objective rational structure.[1] Moreover, Gilkey correctly observes that the Hartshornian metaphysical sled encounters hard going on the contemporary philosophical and religious terrain, because many modern secular minds are unable to assume there is so much rationality to the world. It is assuredly true that there is today a widespread lack of philosophical faith in the universal logos structure of reality. However, if this skepticism concerning reason is really radical, then all genuine philosophical and religious thought is totally undermined, including Gilkey's own important theological work. Many people are not as unrestrained in their confidence in reason as is Hartshorne, but the alternative to *some* faith in rationality is not another philosophy but none at all. Either one must share to some extent Hartshorne's "faith in the rights and duties of rational metaphysical inquiry" or he must despair of the philosophical quest.

Furthermore, Hartshorne's stress on change and process as ultimates undeniably highlights a much-neglected aspect of the whole of reality. Modern thought has been dominated by notions of eternal being, natural laws, and scientific determinisms, with the result that man's creativity, hope, and awareness of freedom have been stifled. Moods of helplessness and pessimism have begun to prevail. Process philosophy is, therefore, a much-needed corrective of theological and scientific dogmatisms of eternal truths, fixed categories, and unchangeable permanences. However, it is possible that Hartshorne, in helping to recover the reality of becoming, does not do full justice to the nature of being; and this lack might become the object of further exploration by philosophers. For example, could there be some improvement in the statement of Hartshorne's belief in universal "self-creativity" as an ultimate, especially since this concept can hardly be said to be fully derived from man's empirical experience?

An especially praiseworthy feature of Hartshorne's metaphysics is his positive appreciation of nature or the cosmos. He relates man to his cosmic environment and expresses recognition of and appreciation for man's kinship with nature. Thus he gives man a feeling of self-understanding as belonging or being at home in the world. In addition, Hartshorne, following Whitehead, has furnished our age of pollution and environmental degradation with a metaphysical basis for developing a full-fledged philosophy of environment or ecology. The present ecological crisis is partially the practical consequence of the old Newtonian philosophy of nature as dead, insensitive, and mechanical; and Hartshorne's panpsychism should aid man's efforts to rethink his relation to the cosmos.

Yet there seems to be a slight defect in Hartshorne's treatment of man-in-relation-to-nature. He does not display sufficient realization of the distinctiveness of man in relation both to nature and to God. Hopefully, in further work he may yet strengthen this facet of his philosophy so as to give adequate recognition to the distinctly human features of man's existence. To be sure, man is kin to the cosmos; but he is also *very different* from all other entities either natural or divine. Both human personality and human history are notions inadequately developed in Hartshorne's writings. In the case of human personal identity, obviously, Hartshorne has not said the last word, although he has significantly illuminated portions of the topic that had

A CRITICAL EVALUATION OF HARTSHORNE'S PHILOSOPHY   *107*

been overlooked. Many thinkers will find his unitary or wholistic view of man a definite asset, and all those troubled by extreme behavioristic and materialistic views of man will be enheartened by his unyielding insistence on man's irreducibly spiritual nature.

An important related characteristic of Hartshorne's philosophy is its emphasis upon aesthetics and the experience of beauty as inherent dimensions of cosmic and human reality. For this feature also he earns our gratitude. It is especially relevant for man in the modern age when science has robbed nature of much of its intrinsic beauty and Protestantism has denigrated the spiritual significance of man's sensitive appreciation of our strikingly beautiful world.

In addition, we should mention Hartshorne's philosophical interest in Buddhism and other Eastern philosophies. This interest marks him as a truly catholic-minded philosophical spirit at a time when many thinkers endeavor to pursue philosophy from a narrowly parochial perspective. Possibly Hartshorne's example will give support to the efforts of some to liberate philosophy from its exclusively Western cocoon into a wider world of global human concerns and needs.

There are, of course, some unsolved problems and paradoxical elements in Hartshorne's metaphysics, and he has candidly acknowledged them himself. We call attention to three such problems.

First, it is strange that process philosophy insists that all of the past is eternally real and "given" (for God, at least) in its entirety, whereas almost all of the past's vast complexity is totally inaccessible to man. Obviously, the given character of all the past is not an empirically derived notion, and one wonders whether it is really indispensable for metaphysics. Many men would like to think that much of the past is both gone and forgotten, and Hartshorne has not fully persuaded me that God could not possibly feel the same way.

Secondly, there is an infinite regress entailed by the idea that every actual event is partially determined by a previous event. Accordingly, there literally never was a truly first event, and the world has had no beginning; the universe thus becomes an actually infinite reality with all the paradoxicalities involved in such a conception. This puzzle is directly related to the problem many theologians have with Hartshorne on account of his explicit denial of the doctrine of *creatio ex nihilo* or "creation out of nothing." It would appear that, without a "creation out of nothing," Hartshorne will continue to have great difficulty adequately allowing for God's transcendence of the world. Nevertheless, every thoroughgoing metaphysics must assume or assert some eternal reality or realities, whether it be God in classical theism or the material universe in Marxism or the God-inclusive-of-the-world of Hartshorne.

In the third place, Hartshorne acknowledges a particularly thorny problem concerning the possibility of relations between entities in the present.[2] Cannot two subjects both know each other in the present and thus determine each other's reality to some extent? In order to answer this query, it seems that all one needs to do is to gaze intently and directly into someone else's eyes. Yet process philosophy maintains that one entity, the object, must be completely unaffected by the knowledge relation.

This enigma is related to the puzzle that relativity physics poses for Hartshorne's thesis. Modern relativity physics holds that there may be a definite cosmic past and a definite cosmic future but not a definite present. However, Hartshorne's philosophy sharply distinguishes between a fully determinate past and the indeterminate future, and this sharp distinction seems to require a definite cosmic present as the razor's edge between the past and the future.[3] Apparently, God must have an objectively right frame of reference from which to determine the simultaneous present; but, of course, the notion of God has no place in physics.

The modern theory of relativity rests on the assumption that light always travels with a finite velocity; but, if it traveled with instantaneous or infinite velocity, there would be a place in physics for the idea of the present as the absolute simultaneity of certain events. Moreover, Hartshorne believes that God, as omnipresent, is instantaneously aware of all events as they occur in the universe. That is, for Hartshorne communication between God and the world is not subject to the same limitation as is communication between man and the world, namely, the limitation imposed by the finite velocity of light. Like Hartshornian metaphysics, Newtonian physics had an absolute present time, because Newton implicitly postulated God as the central cosmic observer of all natural events.

Nevertheless, Hartshorne's ideas do not necessarily conflict with physics, inasmuch as the whole notion of God fits nowhere into physical theories; but they do exceed or supplement what physics is able to conceptualize. The question seems to be entirely one of the validity of non-empirical metaphysical insights. Does metaphysics have powers of attaining genuine knowledge that is unattainable by ordinary physics? This is the issue. However, most modern philosophy is split into two camps over this very point. Of course, as far as Hartshorne is concerned, he is completely unwilling to allow physics or any other empirical science to fasten a positivistic strait jacket upon metaphysics, although he is perplexed by the special problem of a cosmic present that is necessary for metaphysics and unallowable in physics.

THEOLOGICAL ISSUES

Turning to the more specifically theological elements of Hartshorne's thought, it is beyond doubt that his greatest contribution to contemporary theology and Christian thought is his massive and persuasive insistence upon the divine relativity. His ideas regarding God's responsive involvement in the world, his ever-changing action upon it and reaction to it, and his own enrichment through history and human creativity must surely be accepted by Christians as authentic insights into the nature of the living God. The entire Christian message of creation, judgment, and redemption through Jesus Christ underlines God's gracious and sensitive relationship to the world of his creatures. Hartshorne often suggests that his neoclassical God is much nearer the biblical and gospel message than classical Christian theology was, and on this pivotal point he must be accorded our agreement. A similar estimate must also hold for Hartshorne's affirmation that the God who is lovingly aware of his world must inevitably endure suffering. The Christian message of the cross of Jesus Christ directly involves the clear implication that suffering and tragedy are more real for God than they are for man.

The Vietnams of the twentieth century not only tear nations asunder but also wrench the heart of God.

Another related meritorious achievement is Hartshorne's sustained and consistent interpretation of the entire cosmos of God, nature, and creatures in terms of love. Of course, it is quite possible that the ultimate source of his idea of the centrality of love in the universe is the historic Christian revelation. Nevertheless, few theologians or philosophers in history have more consistently made love a universal category for the interpretation of all existence than Hartshorne has. Although some will want to fault him for making too little of God's justice and even wrath, still they should give patient and careful attention to his efforts to take the idea of the centrality of love with complete seriousness. Obviously, many Christians have only taken this central theme of the New Testament's understanding of God halfway to heart. Hartshorne's writings on this subject, as exacting to comprehend as they are, may have a purifying effect on the minds and emotions of some readers, as this one can bear witness.

Furthermore, Hartshorne might also have enabled Christian theology partially to break the stalemate that has long existed over the problem of evil. His clarity and honesty have enabled him to build a convincing case for modification of the traditional notion of God's omnipotence. It is difficult to see how he could be wrong in declaring that "omnipotence" cannot mean that God is literally *all*-powerful. For instance, almost certainly there are some things that not even God can do for me, such as make *my* decisions for me. Hartshorne's neoclassical affirmation of the real but limited freedom of all creatures may lead to a fresh look at the whole issue of evil of which our century knows so much. Admittedly, it is bad news that Hartshorne postulates that evil will be forever with us and that there is no final redemption from it; but many traditional Christian versions of hell have implied that evil in the form of inconceivably brutal torture and suffering is the everlasting lot of most of the human race!

On the debit side of Hartshorne's theological ledger, he does not appear to accord proper weight to the classically biblical and Christian conceptions of the holiness of God. True, his panentheistic deity does possess a certain degree of divine majesty, but it is attenuated in form. One feels a glaring omission in the lack of any real suggestion of God's awe-inspiring and fascinating mystery such as was depicted so unforgettably by Rudolf Otto in *The Idea of the Holy*. Granted that Hartshorne does occasionally hint that God might be the fire that burns as well as the sympathy that soothes, but this suggestion needs developing far beyond the level of a faint acknowledgment.

Additionally, does not Hartshorne have too optimistic an estimate of man's nature and will? He properly asserts the reality of human altruism in spite of all egotism, but can he account for a stubborn perversity in man's will, i.e., for rebellion against humanity and God? Like Whitehead, Hartshorne has very little to say concerning the biblical and existentialist themes of sin and guilt. Nothing in his thought seems to correspond to Plato's famous portrayal in *The Republic* of ordinary men as cavedwellers in bondage, darkness, lies, and delusions. The history of the twentieth century confirms Plato's judgment and suggests a possible source of information for making Hartshorne's philosophy more realistic about the human condition.

Again like Whitehead, Hartshorne probably overstresses aesthetics at the expense of ethics and morality, even if his philosophy is unquestionably a healthy corrective of gross excesses of the opposite sort. There has been too much moralism in recent interpretations of Christian ethics, at least on the popular level. However, although Hartshorne understands quite well "the holiness of beauty," he is a bit nebulous and confused regarding "the beauty of holiness." May not God's love cause him to make moral *demands* of his creatures as well as appeals to them, especially demands for justice, mercy, and humility? Along this same line, Hartshorne's understanding of worship needs enlargement by the Pauline idea that one's entire life of obedience to God may be an act of spiritual worship and sacrifice.

In seeking to render a concluding evaluation of Hartshorne's theological significance, the most salient feature in my mind is the clear conviction that he is more dependent upon Christian revelation than he admits and that his theology could gain in needed concreteness by a still more explicit appeal to Christian revelation. To take the most important case, where did Anselm obtain his formula for God as "that than which nothing greater can be conceived" if he did not, as Karl Barth says he did, derive it from meditation upon the meaning of the Christian revelation of God? Hartshorne's translation of this Anselmian formula for God is "the Unsurpassable One," which he acknowledges was partly derived from the demands of worship.[4] But whence has the Western world obtained its idea that God is worthy of adoring love and ultimate devotion? It has come from the Hebrew-Christian revelation of the sovereign Creator God who is at work in nature and history for his own glory and for man's good. This is the fundamental basis for the worship of God in the Jewish, Christian, and Islamic traditions. Therefore, it appears that Hartshorne's metaphysical vision is, in a way that he does not fully realize, partially parasitic upon revelation as God's self-disclosure to man.

Accordingly, some of the basic presuppositions of Hartshorne's philosophy are assuredly molded by the Christian vision of reality. Indeed, what is his serene confidence in the objective rationality of the world and the powers of human reason to discover it but an unrecognized expression of the belief that both forms of rationality are gifts of God, the Creator of both man and the world? His faith in metaphysical reason appears to rest upon a prior and more ultimate faith in God. If so, it would not be inappropriate to characterize his thought as similar to Anselm's in being a form of "faith in search of understanding." Though he rightly insists that his philosophy be judged by the standards prevailing in secular philosophy generally, he might be in fact more of a Christian philosopher than he has ever admitted.

For developing our thesis that Hartshorne's theology needs supplementation by explicit appeal to Christian revelation, we may refer to several of his own important statements. He writes:

> The concrete whole we are unable to know, but metaphysics can give us its most abstract principle, and with that, together with fragments of the whole which we get from science and personal experiences, we can be content.[5]

Moreover, he repeatedly affirms that the God of our world and us creatures today cannot be known at all through any metaphysical proof and only partially through science,

Scripture, religion, and personal experience. He also says that, for any knowledge of God beyond "the bare outline of the dimensions of his being," we must look to empirical science and theology.[6] This, says he, is the reason why purely philosophical theology can say nothing about such pivotal religious doctrines as sin, grace, and forgiveness. Moreover, this also seems to be the basis for his assertion that "the highest knowledge is not metaphysical, but empirical . . . ."[7] Nevertheless, he labels as "negligibly small" our total knowledge of divine reality gained from all the available empirical sources.[8]

Such assertions as those just cited appear to be Hartshorne's clear confession that, in order to be supremely interesting for man, his metaphysical knowledge of God requires supplementation from empirical sources, including Christian revelation. And if this is a legitimate interpretation of the meaning of such statements, then there seems to be no irresolvable conflict between Hartshorne's metaphysical God and Karl Barth's triune God who is only known through his self-disclosure to the world through Jesus Christ and the Holy Spirit. Furthermore, if Barth's God is correlated with the *concrete* aspects of Hartshorne's God, then it also seems that Hartshorne must agree with Barth's dictum that theological knowledge of God can gain nothing from metaphysics. A parallel statement from Hartshorne would be something to the effect that God's concrete actuality is not deducible from his abstract essence or from his previous actualities.

It is somewhat ironical to suggest that Hartshorne's God is lacking in concreteness; but, at least from the standpoint of Christian theology, this is precisely the verdict that has been reached. And it seems that Hartshorne might

be willing to acknowledge the justice of the decision. Besides the statements quoted above, he confesses that he has
very little to say about Christology and is genuinely perplexed by such traditionally Christian ideas as individual
survival after death and petitionary prayer.[9] May not the
Christian revelation of God as Father, Son, and Spirit,
illuminate his darkness and ours about these and other
enigmatic mysteries? Are there not some points of identity
between the God of Hartshorne's philosophy and the God
and Father of our Lord Jesus Christ?

Notes

Chapter I

1. Charles Hartshorne, *Man's Vision of God and the Logic of Theism* (Chicago: Willett, Clark & Co., 1941), p. xviii.
2. Ralph E. James, *The Concrete God: A New Beginning for Theology—The Thought of Charles Hartshorne* (Indianapolis: The Bobbs-Merrill Company, 1967). Part I provides a useful analysis of the influence upon Hartshorne of Husserl, Heidegger, Charles Sanders Peirce, and Alfred North Whitehead.
3. Charles Hartshorne, *The Logic of Perfection and Other Essays in Neoclassical Metaphysics* (LaSalle, Ill.: Open Court Pub. Co., 1962), pp. viii–ix.
4. Ibid.
5. *Man's Vision of God*, p. xviii.
6. Charles Hartshorne, *Reality as Social Process: Studies in Metaphysics and Religion* (Glencoe, Ill.: The Free Press; Boston: Beacon Press, 1953), pp. 19–23.

Chapter II

1. *Reality as Social Process*, p. 174.
2. Charles Hartshorne, *Beyond Humanism: Essays in the Philosophy of Nature* (Chicago: Willett, Clark & Co., 1937), p. 260.
3. Alfred North Whitehead, *Process and Reality: An Essay in Cosmology* (New York: Harper & Row, 1960), p. 4.
4. *The Logic of Perfection*, p. 285.
5. Charles Hartshorne, "Metaphysical Statements as Nonrestrictive and Existential," *The Review of Metaphysics* 12 (September 1958): 37, 42.
6. *The Logic of Perfection*, p. 288.
7. Ibid., (italics his).
8. *Reality as Social Process*, pp. 175–76.
9. Charles Hartshorne, "Panpsychism," in *A History of Philosophical Systems*, ed. Vergilius Ferm (New York: The Philosophical Library, 1950), p. 450.
10. Ibid., pp. 450–51.
11. Whitehead, *Process and Reality*, pp. 27–28.

12. Charles Hartshorne, "Introduction: The Development of Process Philosophy," in *Philosophers of Process*, ed. Douglas Browning (New York: Random House, 1965), p. xviii.

13. *Reality as Social Process*, p. 44.

14. Ibid.

15. *The Logic of Perfection*, p. 219.

16. Ibid., p. 218.

17. Charles Hartshorne, *The Philosophy and Psychology of Sensation* (Chicago: The University of Chicago Press, 1934), p. 16.

18. *Beyond Humanism*, pp. 183, 185.

19. *The Philosophy and Psychology of Sensation*, pp. 208, 13–14.

20. Ibid., p. 247.

21. Ibid., pp. 269–70.

22. "Panpsychism," p. 442.

23. Ibid., p. 445.

24. Ibid., pp. 442, 445.

25. *The Philosophy and Psychology of Sensation*, p. 269.

26. *The Logic of Perfection*, pp. 123–26.

27. *Beyond Humanism*, p. 121.

28. Ibid., p. 236.

29. Ibid., p. 166.

30. Ibid., pp. 190, 177, 191.

31. *Reality as Social Process*, pp. 69–70.

32. Ibid., p. 84.

33. "Panpsychism," p. 451.

34. *The Logic of Perfection*, p. 191.

35. Ibid., p. 192.

36. Ibid., p. 193.

37. *Reality as Social Process*, p. 62.

38. *The Logic of Perfection*, p. 196.

39. Ibid., p. 204.

40. Ibid., pp. 196–98, 204.

41. Ibid., p. 193.

42. Ibid., p. 200.

43. *Reality as Social Process*, p. 38.

44. "Introduction: The Development of Process Philosophy," pp. vi–vii.

45. Ibid., pp. xiv, xvi–xix.

46. Ibid., p. xxii.

47. Charles Hartshorne, "time," in *An Encyclopedia of Religion*, ed. Vergilius Ferm (New York: The Philosophical Library, 1945), pp. 787–88; *Reality as Social Process*, p. 75.

48. "time," pp. 787–88; *Beyond Humanism*, p. 174.

49. *The Logic of Perfection*, p. 248.

50. *Beyond Humanism*, pp. 135–38.

51. *The Logic of Perfection*, pp. 246, 249–52.

52. "time," pp. 787–88.

53. *The Logic of Perfection*, pp. 5, 12–14.

54. Ibid., p. 14.

55. *Beyond Humanism*, p. 150.

56. *The Logic of Perfection*, chap. 6.

57. *Beyond Humanism*, pp. 163–64.

58. Ibid., p. 156; *Reality as Social Process*, pp. 87–89.

59. *The Logic of Perfection*, pp. 230–33.

60. Ibid., p. 231.

61. Cf. especially *The Logic of Perfection*, chap. 6, and *Beyond Humanism*, chap. IX. Interestingly, Hartshorne does affirm that the present fully determines or logically implies the *past* but not, of course, the future. Cf. *Beyond Humanism*, p. 138.

62. *Beyond Humanism*, p. 131.

63. Ibid., pp. 132–33 (italics his).

Chapter III

1. See "Introduction: The Development of Process Philosophy," p. xxi.

2. *Reality as Social Process*, p. 102.

3. Cf. *The Logic of Perfection*, pp. 20, 122.

4. Ibid., pp. 219–20.

5. "Introduction: The Development of Process Philosophy," p. xii.

6. Ibid., p. xxi.

7. Ibid., p. xii.

8. *Reality as Social Process*, p. 102.

9. Ibid., p. 209.

10. Ibid., p. 210.

11. *The Logic of Perfection*, p. 221.

12. Ibid.

13. Ibid., p. 201.

14. *Reality as Social Process*, p. 57.

15. Ibid., p. 36.

16. Ibid., p. 37.

17. Ibid., p. 103.

18. Cf. *Beyond Humanism*, p. 29.

19. Cf. *Man's Vision of God*, p. 188.

20. Ibid., p. 179 (italics his).

21. Ibid., p. 183.

22. Ibid.

23. See above, pp. 32–33.

24. *Beyond Humanism*, p. 199.

25. Ibid., pp. 199–205.

26. Ibid., p. 197.

27. *Man's Vision of God*, pp. 186–90.

28. *Reality as Social Process*, p. 136.

29. Ibid., p. 209.

30. *The Logic of Perfection*, p. 18.

31. *Reality as Social Process*, pp. 63–64.

32. Ibid., p. 65; *The Logic of Perfection*, pp. 16–17. Cf. also *Beyond Humanism*, pp. 32–34.

33. *The Logic of Perfection*, p. 310.

34. Ibid., pp. 145–46; *Reality as Social Process*, pp. 60–65.

35. *Beyond Humanism*, p. 156.

36. Ibid., pp. 29–30; *Reality as Social Process*, p. 108.

37. *The Logic of Perfection*, p. 129.

38. Ibid., p. 130.

39. *Reality as Social Process*, p. 108.

40. Ibid., p. 103.

41. Ibid., pp. 213–15.

42. Ibid., pp. 41, 212; *The Logic of Perfection*, pp. 242, 251–52.

43. Cf. *Reality as Social Process*, pp. 143, 211.

44. *The Logic of Perfection*, pp. 243, 253.

45. Ibid., p. 254.

46. Ibid., pp. 254–56.

47. *Reality as Social Process*, pp. 42, 143, 211.

48. *The Logic of Perfection*, p. 259.

49. Ibid., pp. 247, 250, 260.

50. Ibid., pp. 243, 259.

51. Ibid., pp. 239–40, 244.

52. Ibid., p. 262.

Chapter IV

1. *The Logic of Perfection*, p. 132.

2. Ibid., p. 131.

3. Ibid., p. xiv.

4. Cf. *Reality as Social Process*, pp. 180–81.

5. *Beyond Humanism*, pp. 2–3.

6. Ibid., pp. 52, 93.

7. Ibid., p. 59.

8. Ibid., p. 106.

9. Ibid., pp. 43–45.

10. Ibid., pp. 12–38.

11. Ibid., p. 29.

12. *The Logic of Perfection*, p. 159.

13. Ibid., p. 152.

14. Ibid., p. 153.

15. Ibid., pp. 150–59.

16. For interesting documentation and interpretation of this phase of development in Western theism, see Charles Hartshorne and William L. Reese, *Philosophers Speak of God* (Chicago and London: The University of Chicago Press, 1953), chap. III.

17. Charles Hartshorne, *Man's Vision of God and the Logic of Theism* (Hamden, Connecticut: Archon Books, 1964), p. 11.

18. Ibid., pp. 85–138.

19. Ibid., pp. 106–107, 109, 117–18, 135.

20. Ibid., p. 89.

21. Ibid., pp. 96, 112.

22. Ibid., pp. 97–104.

23. Ibid., pp. 14, 115.

24. Ibid., pp. 13, 135.

25. Charles Hartshorne, *The Divine Relativity: A Social Conception of God* (New Haven and London: Yale University Press, 1948), pp. 116–17.

26. Ibid., pp. 1, 5.

27. See Charles Hartshorne, "Metaphysics in North America," in *Contemporary Philosophy: A Survey*, ed. Raymond Klibansky (Florence: La Nuova Italia Editrice, 1969), pp. 40–41.

28. *The Divine Relativity*, pp. 80–81.

29. Charles Hartshorne, "Is God's Existence a State of Affairs?" in *Faith and the Philosophers*, ed. John Hick (New York: St. Martin's Press, Inc., 1964), pp. 26–27, 31–32.

30. *Philosophers Speak of God*, pp. 2–3.

31. Ibid., pp. 3–7.

32. Ibid., p. 24.

33. Ibid., pp. 2–7.

34. Charles Hartshorne, *A Natural Theology for Our Time* (LaSalle, Ill.: Open Court, 1967), pp. 127–34.

35. *Man's Vision of God*, pp. 12–21.

36. Charles Hartshorne, "The Dipolar Conception of Deity," *The Review of Metaphysics* 21 (December 1967): 285.

37. *A Natural Theology for Our Time*, pp. 3–7.

38. Ibid., pp. 7–14.

39. *Man's Vision of God*, p. xiv.

40. Ibid., pp. ix, 346–47.

41. "Is God's Existence a State of Affairs?" pp. 28–29.

42. Ibid., pp. 29–30.

43. Charles Hartshorne, "A Philosopher's Assessment of Christianity," in *Religion and Culture: Essays in Honor of Paul Tillich*,

ed. Walter Leibrecht (New York: Harper and Bros., 1959), p. 168.
44. *The Divine Relativity*, p. 8.
45. Ibid., p. 48.
46. Ibid., p. 29.
47. *A Natural Theology for Our Time*, pp. 20–21.
48. *Man's Vision of God*, pp. 347–48.
49. *The Divine Relativity*, pp. 88–91.
50. Ibid., p. 76; cf. *Philosophers Speak of God*, p. 271.
51. *Philosophers Speak of God*, p. 17.
52. Ibid., pp. 513–14.
53. *Man's Vision of God*, pp. 174–92.
54. Charles Hartshorne, "Whitehead in French Perspective: A Review Article," *The Thomist* 33 (July 3, 1969): 578.
55. *Man's Vision of God*, p. 351.
56. Charles Hartshorne, "Psychology and the Unity of Knowledge," *The Southern Journal of Philosophy* 5 (Summer 1967): 89.
57. "The Dipolar Conception of Deity," p. 284.
58. Ibid., p. 288; *The Divine Relativity*, p. 142.
59. *The Divine Relativity*, p. xvii.
60. *A Natural Theology for Our Time*, p. 113.
61. *Man's Vision of God*, p. 230.
62. *Philosophers Speak of God*, p. 15.
63. *Man's Vision of God*, p. 30.
64. "The Dipolar Conception of Deity," p. 285.
65. *A Natural Theology for Our Time*, p. 123.
66. *Man's Vision of God*, pp. 195–98.
67. "Is God's Existence a State of Affairs?" p. 31.
68. "A Philosopher's Assessment of Christianity," p. 173.
69. *A Natural Theology for Our Time*, p. 89.
70. See especially *The Logic of Perfection*, chap. 2, and *Anselm's Discovery: A Re-examination of the Ontological Proof for God's Existence* (LaSalle, Ill.: Open Court, 1965).
71. *Anselm's Discovery*, p. 300.
72. Ibid., pp. 30, 34, 99, 134.
73. Ibid., pp. 3, 43.
74. *The Logic of Perfection*, pp. 38, 149; Charles Hartshorne, "Necessity," *The Review of Metaphysics* 21 (December 1967): 292.
75. *The Logic of Perfection*, pp. 68, 100–101, 108–109.
76. Ibid., pp. 72, 111, 116.
77. Charles Hartshorne, "What Did Anselm Discover?" in *The Many-faced Argument: Recent Studies on the Ontological Argument for the Existence of God*, eds. John Hick and Arthur C. McGill (New York: The Macmillan Company, 1967), p. 322.

78. *Man's Vision of God*, p. 251; *A Natural Theology for Our Time*, p. 53.

79. *Man's Vision of God*, pp. 257–58, 290, 305, 337.

80. *A Natural Theology for Our Time*, p. 59.

81. Ibid., p. 53.

82. *Man's Vision of God*, p. 340.

Chapter V

1. Langdon Gilkey, *Naming the Whirlwind: The Renewal of God-Language* (Indianapolis and New York: The Bobbs-Merrill Company, 1969), pp. 210–14.

2. *The Divine Relativity*, pp. 98–99.

3. *A Natural Theology for Our Time*, p. 93.

4. *The Logic of Perfection*, p. 113.

5. Ibid., p. 15.

6. *Man's Vision of God*, p. 345.

7. Ibid.

8. *A Natural Theology for Our Time*, p. 77.

9. "A Philosopher's Assessment of Christianity," pp. 175–79.

Selected Bibliography

I. WORKS BY HARTSHORNE

An exhaustive bibliography of Hartshorne's published writings from 1929 to 1967, compiled by Mrs. Charles Hartshorne, is included in Ralph E. James, *The Concrete God: A New Beginning for Theology—The Thought of Charles Hartshorne* (Indianapolis: Bobbs-Merrill Company, 1967), pp. 195–223.

A less exhaustive but useful bibliography of Hartshorne's writings, also compiled by Mrs. Hartshorne, is available in William L. Reese and Eugene Freeman, editors, *Process and Divinity: Philosophical Essays Presented to Charles Hartshorne* (LaSalle, Ill.: Open Court Publishing Company, 1964), pp. 579–91.

The following listings are his major books and a selection of his articles.

A. Books

Anselm's Discovery: A Re-examination of the Ontological Proof for God's Existence. LaSalle, Ill.: Open Court Publishing Company, 1965. Also available in a paperback edition.

Beyond Humanism: Essays in the New Philosophy of Nature. Chicago: Willett, Clark and Company, 1937. Reprint paperback. Lincoln, Neb.: University of Nebraska Press, 1968.

Creative Synthesis and Philosophic Method. LaSalle, Ill.: Open Court Publishing Company, 1970.

The Divine Relativity: A Social Conception of God. New Haven and London: Yale University Press, 1948. Also available in a paperback edition.

The Logic of Perfection and Other Essays in Neoclassical Metaphysics. LaSalle, Ill.: Open Court Publishing Company, 1962. Also available in a paperback edition.

Man's Vision of God and the Logic of Theism. Chicago: Willett,

Clark and Company, 1941. Reprint. New York: Harper & Bros. Publishers. 2nd reprint. Hamden, Conn.: Archon Books, 1964.

A Natural Theology for Our Time. LaSalle, Ill.: Open Court Publishing Company, 1967. Also available in a paperback edition.

Philosophers Speak of God. William L. Reese, coauthor. Chicago: University of Chicago Press, 1953. Also available in a paperback edition.

The Philosophy and Psychology of Sensation. Chicago: University of Chicago Press, 1934.

Reality as Social Process: Studies in Metaphysics and Religion. Glencoe, Ill.: The Free Press; Boston: Beacon Press, 1953.

B. Articles

"The Dipolar Conception of Deity." *The Review of Metaphysics* 21 (December 1967).

"The God of Religion and the God of Philosophy." In *Talk of God*, edited by G. N. Vessey, pp. 152–67. Royal Institute of Philosophy Lectures, vol. 2. New York: St. Martin's Press, 1969.

"Introduction: The Development of Process Philosophy." In *Philosophers of Process*, edited by Douglas Browning. New York: Random House, 1965.

"Is God's Existence a State of Affairs?" In *Faith and the Philosophers*, edited by John Hick, pp. 26–33. New York: St. Martin's Press, 1964.

"Metaphysical Statements as Nonrestrictive and Existential." *The Review of Metaphysics* 12 (September 1958).

"Metaphysics in North America." In *Contemporary Philosophy: A Survey*, edited by Raymond Klibansky. Florence: La Nuova Italia Editrice, 1969.

"Necessity." *The Review of Metaphysics* 21 (December 1967).

"Panpsychism." In *A History of Philosophical Systems*, edited by Vergilius Ferm. New York: The Philosophical Library, 1950.

"Paul Weiss's *The God We Seek.*" *The Review of Metaphysics* 25 (June 1972, 25th anniversary supplement): 108–16.

"A Philosopher's Assessment of Christianity." In *Religion and Culture: Essays in Honor of Paul Tillich*, edited by Walter Leibrecht. New York: Harper & Bros., 1959.

"Religion in Process Philosophy." In *Religion in Philosophical and Cultural Perspective: A Cross-Disciplinary Approach*, edited by J. Clayton Feaver and William Horosz, pp. 152–67. Princeton: D. Van Nostrand Company, 1967.

"time." In *An Encyclopedia of Religion*, edited by Vergilius Ferm. New York: The Philosophical Library, 1945.

"What Did Anselm Discover?" In *The Many-faced Argument: Recent Studies on the Ontological Argument for the Existence of God*, edited by John Hick and Arthur C. McGill. New York: The Macmillan Company, 1967.

"Whitehead in French Perspective: A Review Article." *The Thomist* 33 (July 3, 1969).

II. WORKS ABOUT HARTSHORNE OR PROCESS THEOLOGY

A. Books

BROWN, DELWIN; JAMES, JR., RALPH E.; and REEVES, GENE, editors. *Process Philosophy and Christian Thought*. Indianapolis and New York. Bobbs-Merrill Company, 1967.

COBB, JR., JOHN B. *A Christian Natural Theology Based on the Thought of Alfred North Whitehead*. Philadelphia: The Westminster Press, 1965.

———. *God and the World*. Philadelphia: The Westminster Press. 1969.

JAMES, RALPH E. *The Concrete God: A New Beginning for Theology—The Thought of Charles Hartshorne*. Indianapolis and New York: Bobbs-Merrill Company, 1967.

OGDEN, SCHUBERT M. *The Reality of God and Other Essays*. New York: Harper & Row, Publishers, 1966.

PETERS, EUGENE H. *Hartshorne and Neoclassical Metaphysics: An Interpretation*. Lincoln: University of Nebraska Press, 1970.

WILLIAMS, DANIEL DAY. *God's Grace and Man's Hope*. New York: Harper & Bros., Publishers, 1949.

———. *The Spirit and the Forms of Love*. New York: Harper & Row, Publishers, 1968.

B. Articles

BEARDSLEE, WILLIAM A. "Hope in Biblical Eschatology and in Process Theology." *Journal of the American Academy of Religion* 38 (September 1970): 227–39.

BIRCH, CHARLES. "Participatory Evolution: The Drive of Creation." *Journal of the American Academy of Religion* 40 (June 1972): 147–63.

KUNTZ, PAUL GRIMLEY. "The Ontological Argument and 'God Is Dead': Some Questions about God; Ways of Logic, History, and Metaphysics in Answering Them," *Journal of the American Academy of Religion* 38 (March 1970): 55–78.

TOWN, EDGAR A. "Metaphysics as Method in Charles Hartshorne's Thought." *The Southern Journal of Philosophy* 6 (Fall 1968): 125–42.